STRENGTH
FOR THE
JOURNEY

DR. JAMES P. POROWSKI

DR. PAUL B. CARLISLE

LifeWay Press®
Nashville, Tennessee

© Copyright 1999 • LifeWay Press®
All rights reserved
Second printing November 2003

ISBN 0-7673-9105-5

Dewey Decimal Classification: 616.85
Subject Heading: DEPRESSION (PSYCHOLOGY)

This book is the text for course CG-0478 in the subject area
Personal Life in the Church Growth Study Plan.

Unless otherwise indicated, Scripture quotations are from the Holy Bible,
New International Version, copyright © 1973, 1978, 1984
by International Bible Society.

Scripture quotations marked NKJV are from the Holy Bible,
New King James Version. Copyright © 1979, 1980, 1982,
Thomas Nelson, Inc., Publishers.

Scripture quotations marked *The Message* are from *The Message*.
Copyright © 1993, 1994, 1995. Used by permission of
NavPress Publishing Group.

Scripture reference marked TLB are taken from *The Living Bible*.
Copyright ©Tyndale House Publishers, Wheaton, Illinois, 1971.
Used by permission.

Printed in the United States of America

Leadership and Adult Publishing
LifeWay Church Resources
One LifeWay Plaza
Nashville, TN 37234-0175

CONTENTS

CONTENTS CONTINUED

AUTHORS

Dr. James P. Porowski is a licensed psychologist with a doctorate in clinical psychology and holds a master's degree (Th.M.) from Dallas Theological Seminary. Dr. Porowski is a professor of pastoral care and counseling at Southeastern Baptist Theological Seminary and the Director of Family Life Resources, Inc. a counseling center in Raleigh, North Carolina. He and his wife Ginny have four children and live in Raleigh, NC.

Dr. Paul B. Carlisle is a marriage and family counselor with a doctorate from East Texas State University in marriage and family therapy. Dr. Carlisle is a professor of pastoral care and counseling at Midwestern Baptist Theological Seminary and speaks regularly on marriage, family, and counseling issues. He and his wife Terri have two children and live in Kansas City, MO.

INTRODUCTION

Welcome to *Strength for the Journey: A Biblical Perspective on Discouragement and Depression.* You may be a person who has struggled or is struggling with discouragement or depression, or you may be one who wants to understand and minister to others who do. Either way, thank you for joining us as we consider a most important life issue.

One of us (Paul) has personally struggled with depression. Paul will be telling his story at appropriate times during the study. Through his counseling practice, Jim has worked with many who have struggled with discouragement and depression while undertaking their journeys with Christ.

We believe the biblical answer for the person who feels discouraged or depressed is hope. This study focuses on understanding depression: what it is, what causes it, and how individuals can discover hope and healing in their walk with Jesus Christ.

This study focuses attention on the important role of hope in overcoming discouragement and depression and points readers to the God of hope for much needed answers. Depression continues to be the number one emotional problem. It is our desire that this study will be a helpful tool for pastors, group leaders, counselors, and concerned individuals as they seek to gain personal insight and to minister to people in need.

Goals for the Study

Please take a moment to consider specific goals for this study. Our desire is for this study to help you:

- understand depression, its causes and its symptoms
- discover the role hopelessness plays in discouragement and depression
- recognize the importance of hope in facing and overcoming depression
- understand how biblical characters looked to the God of hope in facing and overcoming discouragement and depression
- learn to apply biblical principles for those who face depression
- understand a biblical model for healing.

Getting the Most from the Course

Strength for the Journey is not designed for you to merely understand concepts. The purpose of this material is life change. *Strength for the Journey* is part of the LIFE® Support Series. This series is an educational system of resources for study groups and support groups to provide Christian ministry and emotional support to individuals in the areas of social, emotional, and physical need. These resources deal with such life issues as chemical dependency, codependency, recovery from sexual abuse, eating disorders, divorce recovery, and how to grieve the losses of life.

LIFE® Support Series courses are a form of focused discipleship. They represent a chance to focus your Christian discipleship directly on specific life issues. The Christ-centered recovery process helps people resolve painful issues so they can effectively minister to others.

Strength for the Journey is an integrated course of study—it combines personal study, interactive learning activities, and group interaction. To achieve the full benefit of this study, you will need to prepare your individual assignments and participate in the group sessions. This is not a course which you will study and forget. It represents an opportunity to understand yourself and others.

Study Tips

We encourage you to study the lessons daily. Five daily lessons compose a week. Studying them daily will give you more time to apply the truths to your life. On the other hand, if you are presently experiencing depression, you may have difficulty concentrating. If you cannot complete five days in a week, do not shame or pressure yourself for needing to go slowly. Your group may decide to take a longer time to study each unit. Do not become discouraged if you cannot complete *Strength for the Journey* in 9 weeks. Remember that the purpose is life change, not speed-reading.

Some of us come from backgrounds, even in our Christian faith, that lead us to believe that we are not truly faithful or Christian if we do not find immediate answers to all of our problems.

As you study, you will encounter learning activities. These activities give you a chance to interact with the truths and principles in *Strength for the Journey*. These activities will look like the following:

In the margin read what Paul had to say about weakness in 2 Corinthians 12:7-10. Below write in your own words Paul's conclusion about weakness:

_____

Strength for the Journey is like having a personal tutor. Study it as if we were sitting with you. When we give you an assignment, you will benefit most by writing your response (as you have just done). Each assignment is indented and appears in boldface type. Lines, such as the ones above, will appear for you to use in writing your answer, but you may also use your own paper. No one will ever ask you to turn in an assignment or ask to see it. You may voluntarily show your work to someone if you wish.

In most cases your "personal tutor" will give you some feedback about your response. For example, you may see a suggestion about what you might have written. In the example above you may have written that weakness is normal or that weakness can, when submitted to God, glorify Him. This process is designed to help you learn the material and apply the concepts more effectively. Do not deny yourself valuable learning by skipping the learning activities.

At times you will be asked to respond in non-written fashion—for example, by thinking about or praying about a matter. This type of assignment will look like this:

Pause now to pray and thank God for unconditionally accepting you.

Set a definite time and select a quiet place where you can study with little interruption. Keep a Bible available for times in which the study directs you to locate Scripture passages. Make notes of problems, questions, or concerns that arise as you study. You will discuss many of these during your group sessions.

Group Session

You will benefit most from *Strength for the Journey* if once a week you attend a group session. Others in your group will share your journey with you. They will affirm, encourage, and love you as you grow. Many of us have experienced problems that leave us with difficulty talking, being honest, and trusting others. You will have to practice talking, being honest, and trusting. The intimacy of your group will increase from week to week as you develop these skills. Your group can become a supportive family.

If you are not involved in a *Strength for the Journey* group, I encourage you to seek out a Christ-centered group. You will find that growth occurs more quickly when you participate in a group.

Strength for the Journey includes guidance for the group leader or facilitator. These leader helps begin on page 153. Do not attempt to conduct a group without studying the facilitator's guide.

Strength for the Journey is written with the assumption that you already have received Jesus Christ as your Savior and Lord and that He is guiding you in the healing process. If you have not yet made the important decision to receive Christ, discuss this with a Christian friend or pastor. On pages 34-36 you will find more information about receiving Jesus Christ as your Savior and Lord. You will benefit far more from *Strength for the Journey* if you have Jesus working in your life and guiding you in the process.

TO THE READER

Perhaps you've tended to back away from discussions on discouragement and depression. Such a reaction is a fairly normal response regardless of whether you've experienced long bouts with discouragement or nights in the dark valley of depression. Most of us would just as soon focus on brighter days!

In my work as a psychologist, I have experienced a great deal of joy specializing in the treatment of discouragement and depression. I have been encouraged day after day by supporting people who wrestle with discouragement.

Many Christians believe life should be problem-free. Life without problems would be ideal—but simply is not realistic. Our goals in writing this book are three fold: first, to help people who suffer from discouragement and depression; second, to provide a resource for those who would like to help friends and loved-ones who struggle; and third, to demonstrate that God's answer for discouragement is hope.

I trust that these goals will be realized in your life as you grow in your relationship with Jesus Christ and discover the hope that He has to offer you. I pray that you will find Him to be "the God of Hope" (Rom. 15:13).

James P. Porowski

P.S. If you are studying this material to understand and minister to others, you will find that some of the questions may not apply to your experience. Answer them as they fit your situation. Paul and I bless you for your concern and willingness to care for persons struggling with depression.

Week 1
Who Gets Discouraged?

Case in Point

The pastor listened patiently as Joe talked about his continuing battle with discouragement. At one point in the conversation Joe stated: "As a Christian I have Christ in my heart. I pray, read my Bible regularly, and am active in my church. So what is the problem? I shouldn't be discouraged at all! Joyful—that's what I should be! I don't know of any followers of Christ who had an experience like mine."

The pastor allowed Joe to finish pouring out his heart before he gently assured Joe that many others have walked the path of discouragement. "The Bible is full of incidents where God's people not only experienced discouragement, but also felt completely overwhelmed by it," he added. A glimmer of hope crossed Joe's face. He wanted to know more about Bible personalities who battled discouragement.

This week we'll observe how God's great saints were never immune from discouragement, yet they continued to find hope.

This week you will ...
- understand that discouragement does not disqualify us from serving God;
- practice trusting God while facing discouragement;
- plan an effective response to discouragement;
- understand what is meant by clinical depression.

What you'll study
Day 1: Elijah: Overwhelmed and Lonely
Day 2: Paul: Afflicted and Despairing
Day 3: The Psalmist: Distant from God
Day 4: Hannah: Provoked and Disappointed
Day 5: What Is Depression?

Memory verse
"Now may the God of hope fill you with all joy and peace in believing, that you may abound in hope by the power of the Holy Spirit" (Rom. 15:13).

DAY 1
Elijah: Overwhelmed and Lonely

Purpose: To compare your experience with a biblical character of faith who experienced discouragement and depression

Passage: Read 1 Kings 18–19 in preparation for today's study.

Can you think of even one Bible character who led a charmed life?

"You mean to tell me you are depressed? I thought you were a Christian!" Such statements reflect the belief that being a Christian somehow makes one immune to the difficulties of life. Can you think of even one Bible character who led a charmed life? Just like the giants of the faith, people today get discouraged for many different reasons.

Today we focus on an Old Testament character. Elijah had a tremendous victory in 1 Kings, chapter 18. He saw several miraculous things happen: a fierce fire from heaven consumed a burnt offering; Israel turned back to God; justice fell on the prophets of Baal; and a long drought ended. How glorious this experience must have been. No doubt Elijah would have called it a spiritual high.

Describe what you consider to have been a "spiritually high" moment in your life.

_____

_____

Elijah Retreated

This great servant of the Lord ran in the face of a threat!

As you begin reading chapter 19, you will notice a change in Elijah's mood. He received a death threat from Queen Jezebel—one wicked woman—and Elijah knew she meant every word she spoke. So what did this great servant of the Lord do in the face of the threat? He ran (v. 3). Yes, you heard me right! He ran!

Check which of these you consider present "threats" in your life.

- ❏ lack of money
- ❏ marriage problems
- ❏ loneliness
- ❏ loss
- ❏ health problems
- ❏ career difficulties
- ❏ problems with children
- ❏ fear of the unknown
- ❏ intense disappointment
- ❏ other _____

How are you responding to the threat(s)?

_____

_____

_____

Elijah Felt Overwhelmed

The Bible says, Elijah "went … into the wilderness … sat down under a juniper tree" and prayed "that he might die" (1 Kings 19:4). Here was a man who experienced a tremendous victory but now sat in the midst of utter despair and hopelessness. His experience dramatically illustrates a basic fact of life—anyone can become discouraged.

The last sentence in verse 4 reveals the depth of the prophet's hopelessness: "Take my life, for I am not better than my fathers." Elijah felt he had utterly failed at his assigned task.

Have you ever felt like a failure? It hurts deeply to feel you have disappointed yourself, another person, or God. A part of depression is the belief that you have failed and that the future holds no hope for you.

Elijah felt he had utterly failed at his assigned task.

Have you experienced a situation which left you feeling hopeless or with a sense failure? If so, tell about it here.

_____

_____

_____

_____

Elijah Ignored His Physical Needs

Verses 5-7 record an interesting sequence. Elijah slept, ate, drank, and slept some more. We often ignore these basic needs in times of stress. Proper attention to the physical needs of the body is essential to spiritual growth and maturity. As humans we must live within the limitations of the physical body God provided for us. We cannot overestimate the importance of proper diet, exercise, and rest. Care for physical needs is so important that God sent an angel whose only assignment was to help Elijah by taking care of his body.

God sent an angel whose only assignment was to help Elijah by taking care of his body.

Circle the number that reflects your attention to the following areas (1 = poor and 5 = excellent).

Eating Habits	1	2	3	4	5
Exercise	1	2	3	4	5
Adequate Sleep	1	2	3	4	5

What can you do to better meet your physical needs?

_____

_____

_____

_____

Elijah Felt Alone

In 1 Kings 19:10,14 Elijah cried out, "I alone am left." These sad, lonely words reveal the truth that those who suffer feel all alone. When discouraged, we can easily come to believe that we have been totally abandoned by people and by God. *Frightening* aptly describes the icy, cold fingers of loneliness.

Verse 14 reveals the seriousness of Elijah's fear when he said, "I alone am left; and they seek my life, to take it away." He must have been remembering Mt. Carmel when he "alone" stood against the prophets of Baal—and now Jezebel wanted to kill him. Can you hear the fright in Elijah's words?

"I alone am left; and they seek my life, to take it away."

Are you now experiencing, or have you experienced a painful loneliness like Elijah's? Describe what loneliness feels like.

_____

_____

_____

When I (Paul) was deep in depression the loneliness was unbearable. Nothing or nobody could comfort my deep sense of abandonment. It felt as if an invisible wall stood between others and me. No matter how I tried, being with others did not provide relief. I felt like the disciples in John 1—an orphan. The worst part was my inability to sense the Heavenly Father. How I longed for Him to walk with me in the cool of the day.

The worst part was my inability to sense the Heavenly Father.

Elijah felt stung by the unfairness of the situation. In verse 14 he said: "I have been very zealous for the Lord, the God of hosts; for the sons of Israel have forsaken Thy covenant, torn down Thine altars and killed Thy prophets with the sword." Elijah could not understand how he could do something so "good" yet feel so "bad." The circumstances simply did not seem fair or right to this man of God. He felt he deserved better treatment by God.

Elijah's feelings are typical of discouragement; they make no sense at the time. We cry out to God, asking the question: "Why is this happening to me? I go to church, I tithe, I love my spouse and kids, and I help my neighbor! Tell me—why is this happening to me?"

Have you felt the desire to ask God, "Why is this happening to me? After all, I am living a pretty good Christian life." Take a moment to list your "why" questions.

_____

_____

Elijah Was Still Qualified to Serve

Elijah, the servant of the Lord, was at his lowest point. He probably felt nearly useless. Perhaps you've felt the same way. You may believe God has no use for you. In 1 Kings 19:15-17 God assigned Elijah a task. Re-read this passage now.

Elijah's discouragement did not disqualify him from service. God certainly knew that Elijah's discouragement was overwhelming, but God also knew that Elijah was still useful. Rather than disqualifying His children from service, discouragement may, in fact, qualify them to minister in ways they never could before.

Do you believe God can enable a discouraged Christian to serve Him? Circle the word that best reflects your answer.

No!   Maybe?   Yes!

I hope you were able to answer *maybe* or *yes*. Take a moment to tell God how you feel right now. Tell Him you believe you can serve Him in times of discouragement, or ask Him for the faith to believe He can use you. Ask Him to use you in His kingdom as He sees fit. Share this commitment with a Christian friend.

Today we have observed a faithful servant of the Lord who was plunged to the depths of discouragement. Do you remember in the beginning of Elijah's story how it appeared that all hope was gone? Instead, God had a plan: He used a day of discouragement as a vehicle for victory.

God used a day of discouragement as a vehicle for victory.

To which particular feeling or incident did you most relate in the life of Elijah? Why?

_____

_____

_____

DAY 2
Paul: Afflicted and Despairing

Purpose: To identify ways to overcome discouragement, based on the example of a strong Christian leader

Passage: Read 2 Corinthians 1:3-11 in preparation for today's study.

Second Corinthians is a personal letter from Paul to the church at Corinth. It is similar to one you might write to a dear friend. Paul was sharing his heart with a church he loved.

Read the passage below. Underline the words *comfort* and *consolation* each time they appear.

Blessed be the God and Father of our Lord Jesus Christ, the Father of mercies and God of all comfort, who comforts us in all our tribulation, that we may be able to comfort those who are in any trouble, with the comfort with which we ourselves are comforted by God. For as the sufferings of

Christ abound in us, so our consolation also abounds through Christ. Now if we are afflicted, it is for your consolation and salvation, which is effective for enduring the same sufferings which we also suffer. Or if we are comforted, it is for your consolation and salvation. And our hope for you is steadfast, because we know that as you are partakers of the sufferings, so also you will partake of the consolation (2 Cor. 1:3-7, NKJV).

How many times were the words used? ___

Now go back and circle the words *suffering, afflicted,* or *tribulation* each time you see them.

How many times were each of these words used? ____

Read the 2 Corinthians passage one more time. What do you think God is telling us by the many times He uses the words *comfort* and *suffering?*

_____

_____

_____

One thing for sure, we need comfort in this life because we all face problems. The word translated *tribulation* or *trouble* means *pressed together* or *pressure*. This type of pressure can result in deep discouragement and even depression. John 16:21 uses the same word for *tribulation* to describe a woman's "anguish" in childbirth. The word picture of labor pains provides a clear image of trouble: trouble can be overwhelming, painful, and all-consuming. God is fully aware of our tribulations and so He gives us comfort.

Trouble can be overwhelming, painful, and all-consuming.

I (Paul) found admitting I was depressed to be very difficult. What would people think if a seminary prof who taught counseling were to be depressed? For a period of time I was overcome with immense shame. Then finally I did it! I admitted that I was depressed. Some relief came from the confession itself.

I learned to "cry out" to God. I also learned that part of my healing was the "crying out." Voicing feelings to God is often a cathartic experience similar to what one experiences when emotions pour out in a counselor's office. As the crying out continues, the healing begins.

As the crying out continues the healing begins.

God really wanted to hear from me, especially during times of trouble. I would get alone in my bedroom where no one could hear me and then I would cry out to heaven: "God, You are killing me! I can't stand anymore! Please rescue me." And He did. But He didn't rescue me overnight; it took time—healing time.

The Source of Comfort and Mercy

In 2 Corinthians 1:3-7, Paul provided wonderful insight for coping with difficult times. He began by reminding us *who* God is.

List five characteristics that, in your opinion, describe God.

1. _____

2. _____

3. _____

4. _____

5. _____

Now look at verse 3 and read who God is according to Paul: "the Father of mercies and God of all comfort." Did you hear that? God is both compassionate and comforting. He desires to walk alongside you.

God is both compassionate and comforting. He desires to walk alongside you.

How does this description compare to your own description of God? Would you be willing to pray the following prayer as your heartfelt response to God?

Lord,
Thank You for being merciful. I need Your mercy so much today. Not only do I need mercy, but also Your comfort. Please walk alongside me. I must have Your strength. Remind me that You have experienced all that I have or will ever encounter in life. Please allow me to feel Your loving embrace and Your intimate mercy today. Amen.

The Apostle Paul's Hurts

Many people consider the apostle Paul to be a spiritual superman. Surely such a giant of the faith could not be overcome by depression! Look at the words the apostle used to describe his and Timothy's condition while in Asia: troubled, burdened beyond measure, above our strength, despairing of life, having the sentence of death in ourselves. How would you like these words to describe your life? My response: "No thank you!" One author translated Paul's description like this, "we were so utterly, unbearably crushed that we despaired of life itself."

I find great comfort in knowing that those we consider to be super saints have encountered extreme discouragement and survived! Those who have gone before us have blazed a trail of hope for us to follow.

Those we consider to be super saints have encountered extreme discouragement and survived!

If you have felt despair, how deep has it been? Circle the number.

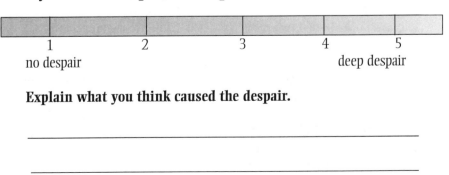

| 1 | 2 | 3 | 4 | 5 |
| no despair | | | | deep despair |

Explain what you think caused the despair.

_____

_____

How much hope do you have today? Mark an X on the continuum below.

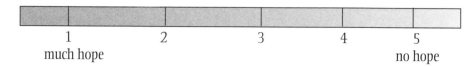

1	2	3	4	5
much hope				no hope

Hope to the Discouraged

So what do you do when you can find no exit from your trouble? Paul tossed us several life vests for use during times of despair. Observe his recommendations for such times:

1. *Tell somebody.*
The apostle Paul told the church at Corinth about his troubles (see 2 Cor. 1:8-9). Disclose your difficulties to those on whom you can depend. Let others know you are hurting.

Let others know you are hurting.

2. *Trust in God.*
Discouragement can produce one of two results: either you trust yourself for help or you grow in your trust in God (see v. 9). Despair easily becomes the victor unless you rely on the Heavenly Father. He longs to help. Call upon Him now and honestly tell Him your situation. Ask Him to provide the faith you need to face your troubles.

3. *Remember God is a Deliverer.*
In verse 10 Paul said, God who "delivered us" and "will still deliver us." The word *deliver* can be translated *draw unto one's self* or *rescue.* God wants to draw you to Himself through the trouble—to be your Rescuer! Recall His past faithfulness and remember He is able to deliver today!

4. *Ask for help.*
Paul mentioned how important the Corinthians' prayers were to him. When you are struggling with discouragement, intimate relationships with God and others are essential. Enlist fellow believers as intercessors and burden-bearers. Share your pain so they can take it to the Father.

> God used some soul-mates to save my (Paul's) life during this time. Two had experienced depression and three had not. What a source of life they were to me during the depression. I could make it through a day if I knew I would see at least one of them. Their presence gave me hope. They did not need to say something helpful, just be with me. I learned how powerfully the presence of another could touch and minister to me.

> **Whether you are currently struggling with depression, have struggled with it, or desire to understand and help those who do, now is a good time to put the principles stated above into practice. Go for a walk. Tell God about your concerns. Talk to Him about trusting Him. Remember the times He has delivered you and people you know about. Then ask Him for help with any issues you are facing in your life.**

DAY 3
The Psalmist: Distant from God

Purpose: To affirm that when we feel distant from God, we can respond to Him in hope

Passage: Read Psalm 42 in preparation for today's study.

Many of the psalms express our personal thoughts, feelings, and dreams. We can quickly relate when the writers declare: "The Lord is my Shepherd" (Ps. 23:1), or "I will give thanks to the Lord with all my heart" (Ps. 9:1). Isn't it great to have a God who cares for us individually and personally? In Psalm 42 the writer described an individual separated from Jerusalem and the temple worship. He expressed his longing for God. He missed the meaningful rituals of the temple. Far from Jerusalem, he felt sadly distant.

Many of God's greatest saints have experienced this sense of being far away from God. The psalmist was like so many people who understand that Jesus is close, but still experience times when they feel painfully distant from Him. Let's look closely at the psalmist's words to learn how he faced this troubling situation.

Many of God's greatest saints have experienced this sense of being far away from God.

Like a tired and thirsty deer (42:1-2)

Read Psalm 42:1-2 below and underline the words or phrases that describe you today.

As the deer pants for the water brooks,
So my soul pants for Thee, O God.
My soul thirsts for God, for the living God;
When shall I come and appear before God? (Ps. 42:1-2)

What do these verses mean to you?

_____

_____

The writer likened himself to a deer, not a camel. A camel is desert-dwelling and self-sufficient. A deer would not survive long in the harsh barren desert because it requires frequent drinks of water to live. The psalmist painted a picture of total dependence on God. He knew that God refreshes and gives life, but he felt distant from the Lord, much like a child separated from his or her parents in a crowd.

God refreshes and gives life.

Recall and describe a time when you felt distant from God.

_____

_____

_____

False Directions (42:3-4)

We see two voices of discouragement. First, the words of the ungodly:

> My tears have been my food day and night,
> While they say to me all day long, "Where is your God?" (Ps. 42: 3).

The ungodly questioned God's faithfulness. They made fun of his dependence on God as if to say, "Where is this faithful God you told us about?" The psalmist was shaken because their taunts matched his feelings and added to his already present doubt. Perhaps in the back of his mind he was thinking, *You are going to come through for me, aren't You Lord?*

"You are going to come through for me, aren't You Lord?"

Name two individuals or groups of people who have negatively impacted your hope in God.

1. _____   2. _____

How did these individuals or groups of people discourage your hope?

_____

_____

_____

The second voice that echoed in the psalmist's ear came from memories of past joys:

> These things I remember, and I pour out my soul
>   within me.
> For I used to go along with the throng and lead them
>   in procession to the house of God,
> With the voice of joy and thanksgiving, a multitude
>   keeping festival (Ps. 42:4).

Sometimes even joyful memories are a source of discouragement.

Sometimes even joyful memories are a source of discouragement—especially when the present doesn't measure up to the past. An unemployed person may experience intense discouragement while remembering a former job that offered a good salary and benefits.

Can you recall a past mountaintop experience in your relationship with the Lord that makes your present circumstances look bleak? Examples may include a former church you attended or close relationships you once shared with fellow Christians. Another example might be a time in your life when you felt closer to the Lord than you do today.

Describe one of these experiences:

_____

_____

Hope in God (42:5)

> Why are you in despair, O my soul?
> And why have you become disturbed within me?
> Hope in God, for I shall again praise Him
> For the help of His presence.

The writer asked himself an important question, "Why are you in despair?" He faced his painful feelings squarely and directed himself toward the only One who could satisfy his thirst. Many of us tend to ignore our feelings, as if denial will force them to cease crying for our attention.

"I really am discouraged!" These truthful words, once spoken, begin the healing process. God heals when we decide not to hide. Like the psalmist, we need to take an open, honest look at ourselves and then ask, "Why am I discouraged today?"

The psalmist's confidence emerged in verse 5 when he declared, "I shall again praise Him." However, this statement does not imply that he never encountered doubts again. That notion is unrealistic and unbiblical.

Christians do encounter problems, and these problems can cause major pain. What transpired in Psalm 42 reflects an emotional tug-of-war. Several times the psalmist indicated he was discouraged and "in despair" (vv. 6,9,11) only to re-assert his hope in God. The psalm ends on a confident note, "I shall yet praise Him" (v. 11).

We ignore our feelings, as if denial will force them to cease crying for our attention.

The psalmist responded to despair with hope in God! Complete each one of the following "hope in God" phrases.

I will hope in God today because _____

_____

I will hope in God today because _____

_____

I will hope in God today because _____

_____

Remember passing notes in school? Here's a chance to do it without getting into trouble. Close today's study by writing God a note. Don't worry so much about making it a formal prayer. Just tell Him what you're thinking and feeling.

_____

_____

_____

_____

DAY 4
Hannah: Provoked and Disappointed

Purpose: When facing our own disappointments, to respond in a healthy way with God's help.

Passage: Read 1 Samuel 1:1-18 in preparation for today's study.

Much of life involves people and situations beyond our control.

Life holds its share of disappointments for all of us. Often our greatest disappointments are focused on situations beyond our control. In fact, much of life involves people and situations beyond our control. Unfulfilled life expectations can lead to a discouragement that destroys hope.

Everyone develops one or more ways to deal with loss. How do you typically respond to overwhelming disappointment? Check the phrase(s) that best describes your response(s).

❑ Give up
❑ Feel paralyzed
❑ Get angry at others
❑ Try harder

❑ Get angry at yourself
❑ Withdraw
❑ Seek help from a friend
❑ Other: _____

Explain why you think you respond to disappointment the way you do.

_____

_____

_____

When life appears to be hopeless, the God of hope is close at hand.

Hannah faced one of life's greatest disappointments—the inability to bear a child. To gain perspective in facing our own disappointments, let's look at how Hannah responded to her agonizing situation. We will discover that when life appears to be hopeless, "the God of hope" (Rom. 15:13) is close at hand.

Hannah's Hopeless Situation (1 Sam. 1:1-8)

Eli's two sons, Hophni and Phinehas, were ministering as tabernacle priests before the ark of God. They are described as "worthless men" who "did not know the Lord" (1 Sam. 2:12).

Although Hophni and Phinehas should have been leading Israel in worship, they stole from the people and were sexually immoral (see 2:22). They represented the spiritual decline of the day and the dark cloud through which Hannah's quiet faith shone brightly.

Like many of us, Hannah faced emotionally overwhelming life situations. Hannah specifically could not control three things in her life.

1. Her marriage: her husband Elkanah had two wives (see 1 Sam.1:2).

Polygamy in the Old Testament was generally surrounded by troubling circumstances, and this was no exception.

2. Parenthood: she was unable to have children, while her husband's second wife, Peninnah, had sons and daughters (see 1 Sam.1:4).
3. Attitudes of others: Hannah was treated with scorn by Peninnah, who deliberately sought to make her life more miserable.

"Her rival, however, would provoke her bitterly to irritate her, because the Lord had closed her womb. It happened year after year, as often as she went up to the house of the Lord, … so she wept and would not eat" (1 Sam. 1:6-7).

Do any aspects of your life feel out of control? Circle the number that reflects how out of control you feel right now.

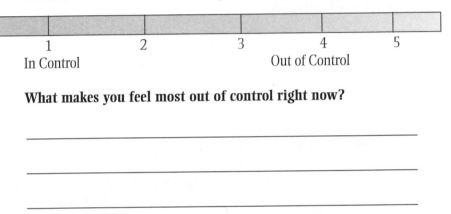

| 1 | 2 | 3 | 4 | 5 |

In Control   Out of Control

What makes you feel most out of control right now?

_____

_____

_____

Would you be willing to pray, like Hannah, and tell God that life seems out of control? Explain how you feel right now. Ask Him to give you His strength to trust Him when much of life seems dark and painful.

Ask Him to give you His strength when much of life seems dark and painful.

Hannah's Response of Faith (1 Sam. 1:9-18)

Many circumstances and situations may be out of our control, but one thing we can control. We choose how we respond to our disappointments. We choose how we react to life's problems.

Eventually, Hannah could no longer take Peninnah's provocation. Hannah's choice was to take her problems to the Lord. She went to the temple to pray. The Bible says that she was "greatly distressed." She "prayed to the Lord and wept bitterly" (1 Sam. 1:10). Take note of how being "greatly distressed" resulted in Hannah's "praying to the Lord." Our problems can serve as bridges to our Heavenly Father. Hannah told God that if He would have regard for her distressed state and give her a child, she would dedicate that child to His service.

Hannah was so overwhelmed as she prayed that when Eli the priest saw her, he thought she was drunk (see 1 Sam. 1:13). Do not quickly draw conclusions about someone facing deep discouragement or depression without knowing all the facts about his or her situation. Hannah described herself to Eli as oppressed, greatly concerned, and provoked (see 1:15-16). This condition motivated Hannah to rest her hope in the only One who could help her. She left her petition with God and "her face was no longer sad" (1:18).

Like Hannah, have you felt overwhelmed with your disappointments? Faith was not easy for Hannah either. It took several years before she reached the end of her rope and poured her heart out to the Lord. If you are facing a particularly difficult burden, one that is out of your control to change, you can control one thing—your response to the situation. Take your disappointments to the God of hope.

Hannah took her disappointments to God. How can you change your response to one situation you are facing? Fill in the blanks below.

Rather than _____, I can _____.
(what you have been doing)   (what you will do instead)

How do you think your life might be different if you change your response to the situation?

_____

_____

_____

Talking with caring friends also helped him to drop some of the shame he had been feeling.

Consider Marty. After experiencing several disappointing situations, he felt extremely discouraged. He responded to his depression with anger and shame. He felt angry because the people in his life did not understand. He felt shame because he somehow thought his discouragement was his own fault. With a Christian counselor's help, Marty learned to change his response to his situation. When he felt angry, he reminded himself that others could look only at the outside; he could not expect them to understand the deep pain of his heart. Instead of remaining angry, he deliberately told close friends how he was feeling. Talking with caring friends also helped him to let go of some of the shame he was feeling.

While God works differently with different people, Hannah gave birth to a son and named him Samuel. We cannot dictate how God will answer the prayers of those unable to have children. Yet, we can learn from Hannah's story that when we are deeply distressed and bitterly sad…

God hears us;
God is deeply concerned for our welfare;
God gives us hope.

Hannah's joyful prayer of thanksgiving is found in 1 Samuel 2:1-10. She praised the God who "raises the poor from the dust, [and] lifts the needy from the ash heap" … to "inherit a seat of honor" (v. 8). She confidently concluded by speaking of the coming Messiah whom the Lord will strengthen and exult.

How could you end your study today on a positive note? Write a card to a friend who is discouraged? Go for a walk? Invite someone to lunch? Write at least two positive action ideas below. Then take specific action on one of them.

_____

_____

DAY 5
What Is Depression?

Purpose: To identify symptoms we might expect to see in a Christian who is depressed

Passage: Read Jeremiah 20:1-2, 7-18 in preparation for today's study.

Looking Back at Days 1-4

In the past four days we have looked at four Bible personalities as they wrestled through their most difficult times.

1. Elijah, a faithful servant of the Lord, was plunged to the depths of discouragement. Though overwhelmed and lonely, God was able to lift him up and use him for further service.

2. The apostle Paul was afflicted and despairing in his ministry. Yet he reported to the Corinthians that the same God who comforted him was also their source of mercy and comfort.

3. A psalmist likened himself to a tired and thirsty deer, as he longed to experience God's presence. Although the taunts of the ungodly and past memories of joy left him in despair, he encouraged himself to "hope in God."

4. Finally, Hannah faced the provocations of her enemy and the disappointment of being childless. She took her despair to the Lord—One who hears our cries and is genuinely concerned for our welfare and gives us hope.

In Jeremiah 20 we read about one of the greatest prophets in Scripture who became so depressed that he wished he had never been born. Jeremiah became discouraged, not from being away from God, but specifically because he was serving God in a difficult situation. All of these examples demonstrate the fact that godly people become depressed.

One of the greatest prophets in Scripture became so depressed he wished he had never been born.

What Is Clinical Depression?

We have looked at five individuals who loved God and yet faced periods of intense discouragement. Some of their experiences revealed thoughts and actions we would expect in a clinically depressed individual. Nearly all people face discouragement at some time. Discouragement lasts for several days, but most individuals gradually begin to feel more positive about themselves and their circumstances. Clinical depression, on the other hand, is a state of prolonged sadness and despair. The following information summarizes the symptoms of depression.

Symptoms of Depression
To be considered depressed, a person would experience five or more of the following symptoms almost every day for a period of two weeks.

1. **Depressed mood** most of each day. Nearly every day for two weeks, person feels sad or empty; cries often.
2. **Loss of pleasure** in formerly enjoyable activities. In a way uncharacteristic for the individual, he or she becomes bored with career responsibilities or faces marital difficulty; cooking or gardening were once enjoyable, but are now burdensome tasks.
3. Significant **changes in weight or appetite.** Person has gained 15 pounds or doesn't feel like eating (a 5 percent change in one month).
4. **Can't fall asleep at night** or wakes up repeatedly throughout the night. May sleep too much.
5. **Fatigue** or loss of energy. Person can't do what they once did; to fix the fence gate or clean the house is overwhelming.
6. **Feelings of hopelessness.** Person experiences worthlessness, guilt, or withdrawal pain in being with others; no light at the end of the tunnel.
7. **Inability to concentrate** or make decisions. Individual may spend an hour on paperwork with no progress. Making simple daily decisions is a chore. Sometimes described as "painful thinking."
8. Recurrent **thoughts of death** or suicide.[1]

"This agonizing pain hovered over me like a black cloud and affected virtually every aspect of my mind and body."

Dwight L. Carlson has been a Christian for 50 years, a physician for 29 and a psychiatrist for 15. In his book, *Why Do Christians Shoot Their Wounded?* he describes a personal experience he had with depression: "More than a decade ago I suffered with severe depression. A patient for whom I cared very much had committed suicide. …

"For over three months a devastating sense of doom kept me feeling desperate and hopeless. It felt like a branding iron in the pit of my stomach, twenty-four hours a day. There was no relief. Though exhausted at night, I would lie awake in bed with that suffocating anguish. When I finally nodded off, a fitful sleep came only for a couple of hours. Then I'd awaken, distressed, only to lapse into another restless sleep. Long before dawn I'd be up again, feeling 'wired,' unable to sleep yet more exhausted than when I went to bed.

"This agonizing pain hovered over me like a black cloud and affected virtually every aspect of my mind and body. Normally I enjoy food and need to limit myself so that I don't gain weight; but during those dreadful months food repulsed me. …

"I forced myself to socialize, exercise and think on positive things; I spent additional time in the Word and in prayer. But I couldn't—by will power alone—shake the depression. It took every ounce of energy, determination and commitment to God to keep me from taking my own life. … Finally, reluctantly, I sought the assistance of a colleague."[2]

This self test gives an individual the chance to examine him or herself. On following continuums mark the spot that reflects your present experience with each symptom.

1. Loss of pleasure in formerly enjoyable activities.

1	2	3	4	5
infrequent				frequent

2. Changes in weight or appetite.

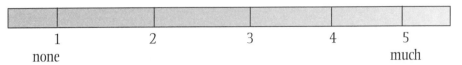

1	2	3	4	5
none				much

3. Changes in sleep patterns.

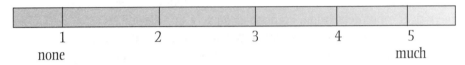

1	2	3	4	5
none				much

4. Fatigue or loss of energy.

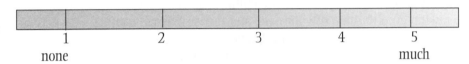

1	2	3	4	5
none				much

5. Feelings of hopelessness, worthlessness, or guilt.

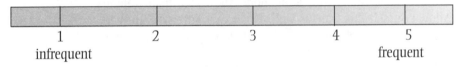

1	2	3	4	5
infrequent				frequent

6. Inability to concentrate.

1	2	3	4	5
infrequent				frequent

7. Recurrent thoughts of death or suicide.

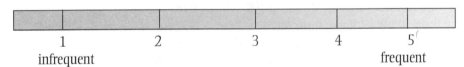

1	2	3	4	5
infrequent				frequent

Check your answers. Did you mark 3 or above on 5 out of 7 of these symptoms? If so, your depression is serious enough for you to seek professional help—especially if the symptoms have persisted daily for two weeks.

A Personal Word from Jim and Paul

Congratulations and thank you for completing the first week of *Strength for the Journey*. Obviously, this topic is one we care about very deeply. Whether you have or are experiencing depression or are studying to better understand and minister to others, we are grateful that you are along on the trek. This week we have studied the prevalence of depression among godly men and women. Next week we'll concentrate on the key element in dealing with discouragement and depression. Researchers have come to recognize that key element as hope.

The key element in dealing with discouragement and depression is hope.

[1]Adapted from the American Psychiatric Association (1994). *Diagnostic and Statistical Manual of Mental Disorders (DSM-IV)*

[2]Dwight L. Carlson, *Why Do Christians Shoot Their Wounded?* (Downers Grove, Ill.: InterVarsity Press, 1994), 9-10, 21-22.

A Letter to the Spouse of a Depressed Person

By Paul Carlisle, Jr.

Dear Friend,

If your spouse struggles with discouragement or depression, you also have a challenging task with which to deal. Your mate needs your support and encouragement to successfully navigate the turbulent river called depression. I cannot adequately sing the praises of my wife Terri. I'd like to share several ideas with you that were a tremendous help to us during my darkness. I hope you can employ these actions along your own journey.

1. *Try to Understand.* Your mate's experience may make very little sense to you, especially if you are not easily discouraged. To even attempt to understand you will have to imagine crawling into the skin of your mate and then asking yourself, "How does he or she feel? What is it like to be in the darkness?" Once you've made this mental journey, attempt to communicate your understanding to your mate. Ask God for wisdom as you share your feelings and understanding.
2. *Slow Down.* During this process it will be helpful to slow your pace of life. For you that may mean volunteering less and being home more. Allow your mate time to think and relax. Allow yourself this time as well. This experience will tire you both—physically and emotionally. Be intentional about slowing down. The benefits will be many and obvious.
3. *Be Available.* Depending on your spouse's experience of depression, at times he or she may want to be alone and at other times to be with you. Making yourself available provides a supportive strategy. Terri's presence was a key factor in my being able to "hang in there" when the bottom fell out of my life mentally, spiritually, and physically.
4. *Find a Friend for Yourself.* We realized early on that Terri needed a good friend to pray and share with who would provide personal support for her. This was such a wise decision on our part. Terri was able to release her frustrations and tension with someone who cared for her which in turn helped to replenish her for the task of walking with me through my period of brokenness.
5. *Pursue Professional Help.* If your mate does not begin to improve in a couple of weeks, seek professional help. A reliable family physician is a good place to start. Do not hesitate to see a psychiatrist or other care-giver if the depression continues. Asking for "help" is a big part of being a Christian. Seeking help is not shameful. The sooner you address the problem, the sooner healing begins.
6. *Never Give Up Hope.* Do not let go of our Heavenly Father, no matter what! At times I would hang onto Terri as she tenaciously held our Father's hand. God *can* provide an answer to the problem. Hope exists—even in the darkest times. God is always there! Hold tightly to Him!

Working through discouragement and depression takes time. It may take longer than you think. I felt some relief in approximately four months, but it took a year or more before I was comfortable with the new way of living that God was teaching me. I realized I had learned to expect instant healing when for me this was a process. Do not be surprised at the length of the process. It is worth it!

In Him,
Paul

Week 2

Hope: The Answer for Discouragement

Case in Point
What's Wrong with Me?

What is wrong with me? Helen said to herself. *If I don't snap out of this, I'm going to lose my job and my marriage.* The words kept coming back to her again and again. Helen doesn't understand what is happening to her. She can't concentrate. She forgets things—important things. She feels tired all the time. In addition, she can't ignore a gnawing sense of impending doom.

Everything seems so hopeless. No matter what she tries, she still feels the same way. She's ready to throw up her hands and say, "What's the use?" At times Helen even thinks, *Everyone might just be better off without me*, but then quickly dismisses the thought. She believes in Jesus as her personal Savior and is a faithful member in her local church. What is Helen to do?

This week's study sets the direction for our study. We want to introduce you to hope—God's answer to discouragement and depression.

This week you will …
  • explain the role hope plays in the healing of discouragement;
  • understand the origin of emotional pain;
  • identify strategies for handling emotions.

What you will study
  Day 1: The Role of Hope
  Day 2: Understanding Emotions
  Day 3: Is God Your Hope?
  Day 4: Seeing the God of Hope
  Day 5: Too Soon to Quit

Memory verse
"For whatever was written in earlier times was written for our instruction, that through perseverance and the encouragement of the Scriptures we might have hope" (Rom. 15:4).

DAY 1
The Role of Hope

Purpose: To affirm the role of hope and faith in overcoming discouragement

Passage: Read Romans 15:4 in preparation for today's study.

We have a simple message to communicate in today's study. Hope is the key to dealing with discouragement and depression. Through all the struggles, we encourage you to hang on tenaciously to the hope that is ours in Jesus Christ.

Hope: the Emotional Component to Faith

Abraham did not believe God's power was limited

"Abraham believed God, and it was reckoned to him as righteousness" (Gal. 3:6). Abraham demonstrated how each of us must approach God by faith. Yet Romans 4:18 describes an important aspect of his faith: "In hope against hope he [Abraham] believed." While everything appeared hopeless, Abraham was still hoping! He did not believe God's power was limited by the aging of his and Sarah's bodies. Sarah was 90 years of age and Abraham 100 when Isaac was born. He still believed that God would give him a son and descendants as numerous as the stars in the night sky (see Gen. 15:4-6).

Have you been limiting God in some way? All of us could use an extra dose of faith. Persons who feel discouraged often think their situations are impossible. They believe there is no way out.

> **Abraham's problem was an aging body. Describe other factors that might make a situation seem impossible.**

_____

_____

Hope is the emotional component of faith.

Faith is not an emotion. Faith has more to do with an act of the will, a choice, but hope is an emotion. In fact, one of the principles embodied in this study is that hope is the emotional component of faith. Hope is faith directed toward the future. We have a goal to present hope as God's answer for discouragement and depression. Romans 15:4 demonstrates that discovering hope involves two important tasks: (1) listening to the encouraging words found in the Bible; and (2) persevering in your daily walk with God. This means hanging in there!

The Facts About Hope and Healing
Through the years medical research has demonstrated the role of hope in the healing process. Consider the following findings:

Kidney transplants: As hope increases, the rate of transplant failure or death decreases.

Treatment of alcoholism: The level of hope experienced by patients was found to be the greatest predictor for eventual success in a study by one major treatment program.

Heart bypass surgery: Patients who had hope recovered six to eight days sooner than pessimists.

Duke Medical Hospital: A recent major study identified optimism as a powerful predictor of who will live and who will die after the diagnosis of heart disease.

The prominent psychiatrist, Dr. Aaron Beck, after conducting his ground-breaking research on hope, concluded that hopelessness is a core characteristic of depression. Later research revealed that the more hopeless persons felt, the more likely they were to attempt suicide.

The significance of hope cannot be denied. The psalmist utilizes this principal as he stirs up his heart toward God:

The significance of hope cannot be denied.

> Hope in God, for I shall again praise Him,
> For the help of His presence (Ps. 42:5).

The psalmist knew that on another day his hope would result in praise. He also trusted that his face would be brightened, since he called God his own ("my God").

Recovery Is a Process—It Takes Time!

Before you run ahead of yourself or another person who struggles with discouragement or depression, remember that recovery takes time.

If you struggle with discouragement or depression, would you be willing to submit to God's timetable for your healing? Discouragement hurts; do not deny the pain. Instead, ask God to empower you to "wait on Him." Right now, write a prayer to God admitting your pain and asking for the courage and power to persevere. If you are seeking to help those who are depressed, write your prayer asking God to give you wisdom and insight.

_____

_____

_____

_____

_____

Abraham often demonstrated hope. He stands out as an example because he maintained his hope in God during difficult times. He continued to believe even when he found himself in hopeless situations (see Heb. 11:11,17). Perhaps you or someone close to you is in a situation that is blocking the light at the end of the tunnel. If so, we pray that this study will help to bring you closer to the "God of hope" (Rom. 15:13).

Abraham continued to believe even when he found himself in hopeless situations.

As my (Paul's) depression deepened and I realized it was not going to just leave in a day or two, I began to read (almost obsessively) about others

Paul Carlisle's story

who had experienced a "dark night of the soul." I drew tremendous comfort—not from knowing others had suffered—but from knowing that I was not alone. I read of great men of God like Martin Luther, Charles Spurgeon, John Calvin, C. S. Lewis, Charles Stanley, and others who battled periods of deep despair. I drew hope from knowing that if God delivered them, I too could be delivered.

How do you feel after reading today's lesson and the portion of Paul's story above? Check your response or write your feelings in your own words.

❏ Encouraged: it helps to know others have felt this discouragement and survived.
❏ Angry: hope seems far too simplistic an answer for me.
❏ Afraid: what if this doesn't work?
❏ Hopeful: I am grateful for the reminder that God cares about me.

_____

_____

DAY 2
Understanding Emotions

Purpose: To develop the ability to identify and admit painful emotions

Passage: Read Psalm 6 in preparation for today's study.

Emotions make up a major part of life. Our standard greeting, "How are you?" is a question about feelings. The other person may reply: "I feel great! What a fantastic day!" or, "I'm feeling pretty down today. Why can't I shake this sadness?" Emotions can't be bypassed or denied. They are an important part of us and demand immediate attention.

So how does a person deal with emotions? Most of us have very little trouble expressing and experiencing good feelings. It's the painful ones that can be difficult. This week we'll focus on those hurtful feelings as we seek to understand them while on our journey toward hope.

Everybody Has Them!

Have you ever noticed how different we are from one another? On the outside we observe tall and short height; dark and light skin; black, brown, blonde, and auburn hair. Yet amidst this diversity, lies a thread of commonality—emotions! Everybody has them! Not a person on God's earth is without feelings.

Not a person on God's earth is without feelings.

Not only do we have feelings, but also, at times, we experience them as negative, painful, and difficult. Some people experience troublesome emotions more than others. If your emotions have been uneven recently, be encouraged. You are not alone in the experience.

Below is a list of common emotions. Circle the ones you experience most frequently. Underline the one that troubles you most.

Sadness	Happiness	Energized	Overwhelmed
Guilt	Peacefulness	Fear	Discouragement
Tenseness	Excitement	Anger	Blue
Calmness	Isolation	Loneliness	Joy
Shame	Other: _____		

The Beginning of Painful Emotions

Emotions reflect our creation in God's image. The Bible describes God with words such as pleased, grieved, delighted, and angry. Genesis 3:10 records the first painful emotion mentioned in the Bible. The serpent tempted Eve to eat of the forbidden fruit. Both she and Adam ate the fruit and then hid from God. Verse 10 is Adam's response to God: " 'I heard the sound of Thee in the garden, and I was afraid because I was naked; so I hid myself.' "

Fear can lead to emotional paralysis. We become unable to think or act. Fear seems to most consistently rear its head in two areas: fear of rejection and fear of failure. When we look at children between the ages of 6 and 10, we can easily recognize these areas of fear.

Emotions reflect our creation in God's image.

Describe a time you feared rejection when you were between the ages of 6 and 10.

_____

_____

Describe a time you feared failure when you were between the ages of 6 and 10.

_____

_____

How do fear of rejection and fear of failure affect you today?

_____

_____

_____

We can hardly imagine Adam's and Eve's relationship to God before sin entered the picture. We have even more difficulty understanding that relationship because we have never shared their experience. Think with me for a minute about their initial relationship with God. First, they felt no painful emotions. Can you imagine? No feelings of sadness, anger, or shame. Such a life is beyond my comprehension! They enjoyed such intimacy with God that they felt totally accepted and loved. They had no thoughts of separation either from God or from each other. However, this oneness changed after the fall.

The entry of sin into the human race gave birth to negative emotions. Never again, until heaven, will humankind be completely free from such feelings. Negative emotions remind us that this world is not our home. Those who have entered into a personal relationship with Jesus Christ will one day be free from the influence of painful emotions. For now we live in anticipation of the day when "He shall wipe away every tear from their eyes; and there shall no longer be any death; there shall no longer be any mourning, or crying, or pain" (Rev. 21:4).

Negative or painful emotions are a part of normal life this side of heaven. We cannot ignore such emotions while here on earth. We can learn to face them, respond to them, and work through them for the glory of God.

Those who have entered into a personal relationship with Jesus Christ will one day be free from the influence of painful emotions.

Don't Deny Painful Emotions!

Be careful! Caution! Watch out! These days a subtle teaching among Christians can prove dangerous and damaging. The false concept weaves its way into the very fabric of American culture. The teaching says when you experience negative feelings, deny them. We see examples everywhere. We often compliment family members for not crying at a funeral. We say, "Big boys (and girls) don't cry." We encourage people to share happy feelings, but then say "you shouldn't feel that way" to people expressing painful emotions.

We can easily understand why people deny negative feelings. Painful emotions hurt! No reasonable person wants or chooses to hurt. So what do we do? We deny our painful feelings and act as if everything is OK. The problem is—all is not OK!

Webster's Dictionary defines *denial* as "refusal to admit the truth or reality."[1] When you hurt and don't admit it, that's denial!

Look at the following case study and underline any statements to which you can personally relate.

Bill did not receive much time or attention from his parents when he was young. He was with baby-sitters more than with his mom and dad. When they did spend time with Bill, they offered mostly negative criticism: "Bill, you are so stupid!" "Bill, why can't you be smart like other kids?" "If it weren't for you, Mom and I would have more fun!" At the time, this criticism seemed normal to Bill because it was all he knew. But as he grew up, he noticed that some parents actually spend time with their kids. He experienced a strange ache in the pit of his stomach each time he saw a mom and dad hug their child. Something in him wanted to scream: "Mom and Dad! Why don't you treat me like that?" Bill's heart was broken.

Eventually Bill grew up, married, and had kids of his own. He could not understand why he got so upset when his wife disagreed with him or why he was deathly afraid that others would reject him. He didn't realize that his past had a tremendous impact on his present relationships. One Sunday during worship Bill's pastor shared how his past pain kept him from developing intimacy with his wife. He explained how he had begun to deal with issues from the past.

Bill was startled to consider the possibility that his past was influencing his present emotions. At first he couldn't believe it, but eventually he assessed the damage of the emotional and physical abandonment he experienced as a child. It took a long time for Bill to admit the pain of the past and begin the healing process. It would have been so easy for him to deny it by saying: "I'm OK. I know Jesus." Bill was extremely thankful for his pastor's courageous self-disclosure.

Reread the statements you underlined. Describe the emotions you felt when you read those statements.

_____

_____

Have you ever tried to submerge a beach ball in the ocean? You could do it, but keeping it submerged would require constant energy and attention. It would also distract you from enjoying other activities that the beach and ocean afford. Now, consider the idea of keeping two balls submerged. The effort would definitely become all consuming and exhausting, if not impossible. The beach ball analogy fits the problem of denying emotions. Consider the results of choosing this strategy:

1. Denial distracts you from living life.
2. Denial is tiring.
3. Denial wastes valuable energy and time.
4. Denial hinders your ability to serve our Savior.

You may be thinking, *Well, what am I supposed to do with painful emotions if I don't deny them?* God has not left you alone to answer that question. Let's look at what the Bible has to say.

Confess and Admit

The psalmist penned helpful words in Psalm 30 that provide insight for dealing with painful emotions.

> O Lord my God, I cried out to You,
> And you healed me (Ps. 30: 2, NKJV).

The verse contains a key ingredient to overcoming discouragement and depression: "I cried out." Consider an infant who cries out to a parent because he or she is uncomfortable or hurting. For the infant, crying is a natural and reflexive response. Such honesty is not always true for adults. Often we believe that denying and hiding our painful emotions is the best way to negotiate life.

Let's take a quick look at one of Peter's encounters with negative emotions recorded in Matthew 14:22-33, specifically verse 30. After watching Jesus walk toward him on the water, Peter struck out across the top of the raging sea to meet his Lord. Then Peter experienced a truly human moment. He took his eyes off Jesus, looked around at the waves and wind, and immediately began to sink. "Afraid" is the word that grabs us in verse 30. What did Peter do when he was afraid? He cried out to Jesus, "Lord, save me!"

Notice what Peter did not do. He did not say to himself, "What will the other disciples think if I am honest about my feelings and cry out to Jesus?" Nor did he

Often we believe that denying and hiding our painful emotions is the best way to negotiate life.

say, "I think I will just stuff this away for a while." He cried out to Jesus. So should we. When the storms of life assail us, we need to cry out vigorously to our Heavenly Father.

Matthew recorded that Jesus immediately stretched out His hand and saved Peter. Hope comes from knowing that God is able to heal and save us from whatever life throws in our path. The psalmist said that when he cried out to God, God healed him.

We know that God does not always respond to our cries in the way or time we might choose. He values our character over our comfort. He views our troubles from an eternal perspective, looking down the road at the result of our struggles. But even if God does not make our lives easy now, we know He always works for our good and His glory. We find comfort in His presence, acceptance, and love.

So when the waves are crashing all around you, or the pain is unbearable, or the emotions are uncontrollable, cry out to God. Admit your pain and hurt. He may choose to alleviate your hurt. He will most certainly embrace you and give you strength.

Hope comes from knowing God is able save us from whatever life throws in our path.

Let's practice "crying out" to God. In the space below record your confession and admission to the Lord concerning any present pain and hurt. "Cry out" to God's attentive ear now.

_____

_____

_____

_____

_____

DAY 3
Is God Your Hope?

Purpose: To determine that God is our hope

Passage: Read Romans 5:5 in preparation for today's study.

June eagerly opened the letter. She had watched and waited for weeks, anticipating a response from her job interview. *Wouldn't it be wonderful to land a job like this right out of college,* she thought. But June's smile disappeared as she read the words, "Thank you for your interest, but we have decided to hire another applicant." She felt as if the life had been squeezed out of her.

Like June, we all experience disappointments in life. Some disappointments are greater than others, but repeated significant disappointment can hammer us to the point that we experience severe discouragement.

The following are some examples of situations that can result in disappointment and discouragement.

- your boss ignores your ability for a job promotion
- your friends exclude you from an outing
- others reject your ideas
- someone laughs at an important and personal achievement
- friends betray your trust

In the space below, describe an event or circumstance you have experienced that resulted in personal disappointment.

_____

_____

One Source of Disappointment

Do you sometimes think that life should be better than it is? Many times we respond to life's problems by saying, "That's not the way things should be!" The apostle Paul explained this mind-set in 2 Corinthians 5:4: "For indeed while we are in this tent, we groan, being burdened, because we do not want to be unclothed, but to be clothed, in order that what is mortal may be swallowed up by life."

Paul addressed the Christian's inner yearning for heaven. He used the word "groan" to describe what happens inside of believers as they anticipate a heavenly home with the Heavenly Father. The groaning results from inhabiting an earthly body ("tent") that is exposed to afflictions and deterioration. He continued by describing life this side of heaven as a burden. The word he used for _burdened_ means "being weighed down by life"—a good definition for disappointment.

Sin has so scarred this world that everyone literally groans and is burdened by life. God did not include disappointments in His original design, yet they punctuate our everyday experiences. The Bible does describe a solution to the problem. Ultimately, God's children will be "at home with the Lord" (2 Cor. 5:8). A day is coming when no more tears or disappointments will cloud our days, but until then, what are we to do?

A day is coming when no more tears or disappointments will cloud our days.

We Find Hope in a Person

First Timothy reveals our primary source of hope. Do you find it surprising that we find hope not in a formula, an activity, or a religious creed? We find hope specifically and only in the person of Jesus Christ.

Hope is found specifically and only in the person of Jesus Christ.

> Paul, an apostle of Christ Jesus according to the commandment of God our Savior, and of Christ Jesus, who is our hope (1 Tim. 1:1).

In what sense can we say that the person of Jesus is hope or gives us hope? To understand the answer consider the following facts of our human existence.

1. We are hopelessly separated from God. Our sin (choice to live life independently from God) has completely destroyed our potential for a relationship with God. Romans 3:23 states, "all have sinned and fall short of the glory of God." Romans 6:23 says, "the wages of sin is death." We recognize that penalty includes both physical and spiritual death.

2. He died for us. Romans 5:8 says, "God demonstrates His own love toward us, in that while we were yet sinners, Christ died for us." He did for us what we could not do for ourselves. Jesus' death made it possible for us, the guilty, to be totally accepted by God. His death, burial, and resurrection afforded us total acceptance by the Father. The Bible refers to God's act as justification. To justify means to declare someone righteous. God pronounces those who are in Christ just as if they have kept the law perfectly.

Jesus' death, burial, and resurrection afforded us total acceptance by the Father.

3. *You have the choice to accept or reject Him.* Just because a gift is extended to someone does not mean it will be accepted or received. One author has said that the Christian life from beginning to end is a life of "receiving" not "achieving." The Christian life begins by "receiving" Jesus Christ as your personal Savior. Read John 1:12, "As many as received Him, to them He gave the right to become children of God, even to those who believe in His name."

Have you made the decision to receive Jesus Christ as your personal Savior and Lord? Put a check before the statement that best describes you:

❑ Yes, I have invited Christ into my life to be my Savior and Lord.
❑ I am not sure if I have invited Christ into my life to be my Savior and Lord.
❑ I have never invited Christ into my life to be my Savior and Lord.

If you would like to invite Jesus into your life, use this simple prayer to guide you.

Dear Lord,
I know that I am a sinner and undeserving of your love and acceptance. I understand that You love me despite my sinfulness and proved this by dying for me on the cross. I open my heart and invite You to come in. I give You my life and ask You to be both my Savior and my Lord. From this day forward I will love and serve You. I so much need the hope that only Your life can offer. Thank You for coming into my life and giving me a relationship with You. I love You Lord. Amen.

If you prayed to receive Christ, one of the first things to do is tell someone else. Who do you know who would rejoice with you that you have become a Christian? Give them a call and tell them what God has done for you. If you are unsure about ever having received Jesus into your life but would like to be sure, pray this prayer.

Dear Lord,
I am unsure whether I ever invited You into my life. I want more than anything else to have a relationship with You, a relationship that promises hope. Please show me if I have genuinely received You into my life. Make it clear where I am in relationship to You. Amen.

If God reveals to you that you do not know Him, return to the first suggested prayer and pray it. If God reveals that you know Him personally, then thank Him for that relationship and ask Him to deepen your intimacy with Him. If you continue to struggle with whether or not you have received Christ, we suggest that you talk with your pastor or a mature Christian you trust.

Hope Does Not Disappoint

The apostle Paul offered some amazingly powerful words to the Romans. "Hope does not disappoint, because the love of God has been poured out within our hearts through the Holy Spirit who was given to us" (Rom. 5:5).

The relationship we have to God through Christ provides us with a hope that will not disappoint. This guarantee does not mean that we will not experience problems, pains, or difficulties in this life. It does mean that we have Someone who will be with us through all that we encounter. He is the One who "sticks closer than a brother" (Prov. 18:24). We need never suffer alone.

The relationship we have to God through Christ provides us with a hope that will not disappoint.

Dear Savior,
I thank You that I have a hope that will never disappoint. How grateful I am that You are my hope! Teach me how to activate the hope You have provided for me. Assure me of Your presence during my darkest hours. Thank You for the darkness because it creates such a hunger for Your light. I receive You as my hope! Amen.

DAY 4
Seeing the God of Hope

Purpose: To determine if you see God as your hope

Passage: Read 2 Kings 6:8-19 in preparation for today's study.

Our culture is deeply rooted in the scientific method. We have adopted the idea that reality is limited to the senses: what can be touched, tasted, heard, smelled, or seen. However, to see the God of hope, we must move beyond our senses.

To see the God of hope, we must move beyond our senses.

Hope Challenged

In 2 Kings 6:8-19 the Bible records that Elisha gave information to the king of Israel that protected Israel from a sneak attack by Syria. The king of Syria was frustrated and angry. He demanded to know who intruded on his plans. "Elisha," was the reply. The king commanded his army to find the tattletale named Elisha.

Even though Elisha was doing the will of God by protecting the king of Israel from the Syrians, he found himself pursued and hunted. His hope was challenged as ours is today. Perhaps those two words *pursued* and *hunted* describe your experience with discouragement or depression. Take heart, the mighty men and women of faith wrestled with these foes as well.

Describe a time that you, like Elisha, felt pursued or hunted. If neither of these words accurately describes your experience with discouragement or depression, choose another word.

_____

_____

The Syrian warriors were well equipped to snare Elisha. They possessed horses, chariots, and a powerful army. Surely they could catch one man! Can you imagine this scene? The enemy completely encompassed the city. They had only one goal: to capture Elisha! Without hope, discouragement surrounds you in much the same way as the Syrian warriors surrounded the town of Dothan. But wait; this is not the end of the story!

This mighty army was the first thing Elisha's servant saw when he went out early in the morning (see 2 Kings 6:15). The servant was so overwhelmed that he said to Elisha, "Alas, my master! What shall we do?"

Eyes That See Hope

Just because one near you is hopeless does not mean that you must be hopeless, too.

Notice an important truth in this story. Elisha had an amazing response, in spite of the fact that his servant appeared to feel hopeless. Just because one near you is hopeless does not mean that you must be hopeless, too.

Elisha's first words to his servant were, "Do not fear" (2 Kings 6:16). Think about those words for a moment. The servant stood before his master horrified at the prospect of being captured by the Syrians. To this frightened man, Elisha said, "Do not fear." Can you imagine the servant's confusion? What was his master thinking? Little does the servant realize that his master will soon confuse him even more.

Elisha announced to his servant, "Those who are with us are more than those who are with them" (2 Kings 6:16). Surely the servant's mouth must have fallen open and rested on the ground. Unbelievable! He had seen no one but the enemy. Should he also be concerned for the mental stability of his master?

Then the servant watched Elisha turn toward heaven and pray: "O Lord, I pray, open his eyes that he may see" (2 Kings 6:17). From this prayer it's obvious that Elisha saw something the servant did not see. So rather than trying to convince the servant of the presence of a heavenly army, he simply asked God to help the servant see. God and only God can open a frightened heart to His hope!

If you would like to have His hope, use the following prayer to ask God to open your eyes to see what no human eyes can behold. Ask Him to let you see and experience His hope.

God of all hope,
I ask You to do for me what You did for Elisha's servant: open my eyes! I turn to You and You only as the answer to my problems and pain. With my eyes I am unable to perceive Your work and Your plan. So I wait on You to open my eyes so they can see. Amen.

God and only God can open a frightened heart to His hope!

If you minister to someone who is depressed, remember the power of prayer far exceeds that of human words. Below write a prayer for someone you know who struggles with discouragement. Ask God to open his or her eyes to the Father's resources.

_____

_____

_____

God opened the servant's eyes, and what he saw was marvelous and awesome. His eyes beheld a mountain covered with horses and chariots of fire. The Syrians had chariots—but not chariots of fire. From Elisha and his servant we learn:

1. *Human eyes are limited.* God has created humans with the ability to see some things but not all things. Our culture is greatly influenced by the scientific method which limits reality to the senses (what can be touched, tasted, heard, smelled, or seen). The problem with this method is that love, faith, joy, and commitment cannot be measured by the methodology of science. To see beyond the physical requires an intimate relationship with God.

2. *God opens eyes to hope.* Elisha's simple prayer opened the door to the servant's spiritual sight. He could then see what God was doing. And with his new sight he understood why Elisha was not overwhelmed by fear.

3. *We can ask God to give us eyes that see hope.* God awaits our request! He longs to impart to us His hope! Ask Him to open your eyes to Him and to His work. Ask others to pray for you as Elisha prayed for his servant.

We can ask God to give us eyes that see hope.

DAY 5
Too Soon to Quit

Purpose: To evidence trust in the Lord for strength to persevere

Passage: Read Isaiah 40:27-31 in preparation for today's study.

Perseverance is one of the great character words in the English language. Success in work, ministry, finances, marriage, and family all depend on our unwillingness to abandon hope.

When I (Jim) was a child, I always admired a small statue which sat on my grandfather's desk. The figure depicted several courageous marines hoisting a flag on a small Pacific island. It embodied the idea that accomplishing dearly held objectives requires a refusal to quit.

People tend to quit when their emotional strength wears thin. What does a Christian do when faced with the temptation to give up? Our study today focuses on this question.

List two times in your life when you were tempted but did not quit.

_____

_____

Looking back at each instance, what kept you going?

_____

_____

Isaiah 40:27-31 provides three essential truths to consider when we are tempted to throw in the towel. These truths promise His strength during difficult times. First, we are never overlooked by God.

God Never Overlooks Us

Why do you say, O Jacob, and assert, O Israel,
"My way is hidden from the Lord,
And the justice due me escapes the notice of my God"? (Isa. 40:27).

God never overlooks or forgets His people.

The people of Israel believed that God did not see their troubles. They thought they were hidden from His view: lost, like a small child in a crowded store. They did not understand that God never overlooks or forgets His people.

Many times we have a tendency to think our understanding of a problem is more comprehensive than God's—that we see things in greater detail and clarity than He does. Perhaps you have made these statements to yourself: *If the Lord had been with me to help, I would have made different decisions. If God knew everything that was going on, surely He would have done something.* Someone has defined a fanatic as a person who does what God would do if He had all the information.

Describe a time when you thought God should do something other than what He seemed to be doing.

_____

_____

If enough time has passed, do you see the circumstance differently now? ❏ yes ❏ no **If so, explain.**

_____

_____

_____

God made life complete with difficulties so that we will learn to focus our attention on the Lord Jesus Christ.

People consider giving up when they limit their solutions to what they can see, feel, hear, and touch (remember yesterday's study?). Relying on sense impressions alone can lead to the false belief that God does not see our predicament clearly. Remember 2 Corinthians 5:7: "We walk by faith, not by sight."

God never forgets about us. From our vantage point, life will always consist of steep obstacles. We will experience times when we have too little time, not enough energy, and limited finances. Yet these circumstances do not indicate God's lack of interest. He has made life complete with difficulties so that we will learn to focus our attention on the Lord Jesus Christ.

In which of the following areas are you currently facing a "steep obstacle"?
❏ Time   ❏ Energy
❏ Finances   ❏ Relationships
❏ Other _____

God Clearly Understands Our Problems

The second truth Isaiah offers us is that God clearly understands our problems.

> Do you not know? Have you not heard?
> The Everlasting God, the Lord, the Creator of the ends of the earth
> Does not become weary or tired.
> His understanding is inscrutable (Isa. 40:28).

The Lord is aware of the difficulties we face down to the smallest detail. He knows the exact best time to act in our behalf. Isaiah described the Lord in three ways that distinctly set Him apart from our limitations.
 • First, He is the everlasting God; He has never changed and He never will.
 • Second, He is the Creator; everything that is exists by His design.
 • Third, His understanding is inscrutable; it cannot be measured.
He is thoroughly aware of every aspect of our lives and is not exhausted by the details. In every situation, God sees the bigger picture. The details of our lives are all within His careful understanding.

In every situation of our lives, God sees and understands the bigger picture.

What is God aware of in your life that you have never given Him credit for knowing or caring about?

_____

Do certain details in your life leave you exhausted? List five large or small stressors that sap your strength.

1. _____   4. _____

2. _____   5. _____

3. _____

Lay those problems, tasks, or irritants at His feet now. Tell Him how you feel. Ask Him to deal with the details. Take a moment to thank God for seeing the big picture.

He Will Reward Our Patience

When tempted to give up, remember the third truth from Isaiah: He will reward our patience with His strength.

The Heavenly Father will reward our patience with His strength.

> He gives strength to the weary,
> And to him who lacks might He increases power.
> Though youths grow weary and tired,
> And vigorous young men stumble badly,
> Yet those who wait for the Lord
> Will gain new strength;
> They will mount up with wings like eagles,
> They will run and not get tired,
> They will walk and not become weary (Isa. 40: 29-31).

The greatest measure of strength is the ability to wait patiently on a sovereign God.

We might say that life is all about strength, and the greatest measure of strength is the ability to wait patiently on a sovereign God. The Lord is speaking to people who are worn out and exhausted by life: individuals so disappointed by the road behind them that they are ready to give up on the future. These concluding verses in Isaiah 40 admonish us that while the best and the brightest may fail, those who wait for the Lord will be strengthened.

Those who wait for the Lord are people who hope or expectantly long for Him to act. They see their circumstances, difficult as they may be, in a new light. The seemingly impossible concerns of life have not escaped the notice of the Lord Jesus Christ. He comprehends every one of our burdens and promises strength and courage to persevere, if we will patiently trust in Him.

When you feel like giving up, take time to review these three important truths from Isaiah, chapter 40.

- God never overlooks us.
- God clearly understands our problems.
- He will reward our patience with His strength.

[1]Frederick C, Mish, editor in chief, *Webster's Ninth New Collegiate Dictionary* (Springfield: Merriam-Webster Inc., 1991), 339.

Week 3

Loss: Grieving Significant Losses

Case in Point

He sat on a park bench with his head propped up by tired hands. He looked like someone had slowly siphoned the life out of him. All that remained was the shell of a man. The look in his eyes clearly said, *I give up.*

What would cause a man to give up? If we were to ask him, he would tell us, with lifeless speech, about his beloved Maria. They were married for 45 years—45 wonderful years. He would describe them as the best years of his life. Then it happened! Three years ago the cold winds of death swept into their lives and carried his Maria away. We would see tears well up in the old man's eyes as he recounts the memories. He would continue talking as if we were not there—totally absorbed in the reality of the past. Finally he would say, "She is gone. Gone. Maria is gone." His voice would trail off into a whisper—and eventually silence.

Loss. We all have either experienced or will experience it. No bridge spans the pain of losing people and things we care about. Eventually we must ford these streams. This week's study will help you or someone you love discover hope while "Grieving Significant Losses."

This week you will ...
- examine one of the five major causes of depression—loss;
- explain the normal, healthy grief process;
- recognize the different types of losses people face;
- identify ways to cope with significant losses;
- discover ways to help others who are having an extreme reaction to loss.

What you will study
Day 1: What Is Normal Grief?
Day 2: Hope in the Face of Death
Day 3: Grieving Your Losses
Day 4: Moving Beyond Your Losses
Day 5: Helping Others

Memory verse
"We do not want you to be uninformed, brethren, about those who are asleep, that you may not grieve, as do the rest who have no hope" (1 Thess. 4:13).

DAY 1
What Is Normal Grief?

Purpose: To explain the stages in a healthy grieving process

Passage: Read 2 Samuel 1:1-27 in preparation for today's study.

Everyone faces grief because life is an extended loss experience. We lose our child-hood, then our adolescence, then each stage of our adulthood. We lose our friends to moves and diverging life paths. Ultimately we lose our health. Along the way many sudden or abnormal losses attack us. In spite of the universality of the experience, loss remains a difficult part of life to endure. Words fail to adequately describe the painful emotions brought on by grief.

Loss remains a difficult part of life to endure.

Perhaps this reality prompted God to provide a picture of grief in 2 Samuel 1:11-12. David and his men reacted in a dramatic way to the news of Saul and Jonathan's deaths. They tore their clothes, mourned, wept, and fasted until evening. David continued to express his grief by composing a song for the sons of Judah in memory of Saul and Jonathan.

"Your beauty, O Israel, is slain on your high places!
How have the mighty fallen!" (2 Sam. 1:19).

Grief means different things to different people. In the space below write your own brief, personal definition of grief.

_____

_____

_____

Webster's offers a helpful definition of *grief: a deep and poignant distress caused by or as if by bereavement.*[1] The definition identifies the two areas of grief we will focus on this week.
1. Grief caused by the death of a loved one.
2. Grief caused by the loss of something else dear to us, such as a job, a home, or a friendship.

Why Do We Grieve?

David responded to the loss of those he loved with deep and moving distress. He expressed intense sorrow over the loss of Israel's king and his closest and dearest friend, Jonathan. David's grief reaction also represented his first step toward healing. In fact, while grief is a very painful experience, the process is essential to accomplish emotional healing.

David's grief reaction represented his first step toward healing.

Our culture, it seems, encourages individuals to hurry grief or to "just get over it." One reason for this may be that our culture does not have time for the slow and demanding grief process. We cannot say exactly how long a person needs to grieve when facing a loss. Grief often lasts much longer than we suppose. For example, many experts say processing the initial grief from loss of a loved one takes two holiday seasons—two Christmases, Easters, birthdays, and anniversaries. Any person who has suffered a major loss can tell you that we continue to grieve for a lifetime. We do get better at coping. We build a new life, but the grief process continues. When we do not allow ourselves to experience a normal grief process, we risk becoming mired in depression, bitterness or anger.

The Normal Grief Process

God created the normal grief process as a way of helping us resolve our losses. For most people it follows a fairly predictable pattern through five stages. However, we do not always progress through the stages in an orderly fashion, never to revisit them again. These stages are more like cycles, like a circular staircase. We repeat each stage time and again but from an elevated perspective if we have grieved in a healthy manner.

God created the normal grief process as a way of helping us resolve our losses.

1. Shock. The first stage is shock. We react with disbelief and even denial when notified of the loss of something or someone we love. Shock protects us from the full impact which initially might be too great to bear. Shock also tends to last longer with a sudden loss than with an expected one. Anticipated loss, as with a terminally ill loved one, or an expected job termination, allows us to do some grieving prior to the loss. Nevertheless, we are still stunned when it becomes reality.

Think for a moment of a time when you have been with someone when they learned of a sudden loss. Describe below the person's reaction to the news. If you have not been with someone in such an instance, describe how you think a friend might react.

_____

_____

_____

2. Anger. Anger is a common reaction to loss. It may be directed at medical personnel, family members, friends, or ourselves. In the event of death, we frequently feel anger toward the person who died. Anger surfaces because hopes and dreams have been short-circuited. The presence of anger may be perplexing for people. Consequently, family members and supportive friends can encourage the person experiencing the loss to express his or her anger in a healthy manner. Unhealthy expressions of anger may include misdirected anger—verbal or physical outbursts at family members—or use of alcohol or drugs. The refusal to express any anger at all is always an unhealthy way to deal with the anger.

We frequently feel anger toward the person who died.

Think of a time when you experienced a significant loss. Did you feel angry? Describe how you dealt with (or denied) your anger.

_____

_____

3. What If? Some refer to this stage as bargaining. We run endless questions through our minds: *How could things have been different? What if I had notified the doctor more quickly? What if I had refused to let her drive to the store? What if I had done my job more efficiently?*

"Why did this have to happen?"

These questions typify the feeling of powerlessness reflected when we ask, "Why did this have to happen?" This stage of the grief process can be observed in John 11:21 and 32. Mary and Martha faced this same question at the loss of their brother Lazarus. Martha said to Jesus, "Lord, if You had been here, my brother would not have died."

Often when we look back at this stage of grief, we realize we thought things that were downright silly. Can you think of an example of bargaining thinking when you experienced this stage of grief? ❑ yes ❑ no If so, describe the "deal" you tried to strike with God or with yourself.

_____

_____

_____

4. Depression. Sadness is perhaps the most common emotion experienced during the grief process. When we lose someone or something important to us, we feel sad. Sadness is both normal and healthy. In fact, counselors do not consider this sad feeling to be a clinical form of depression. It is a normal reaction to loss. This type of depression indicates that something very valuable and precious was lost. In a sense, depression reveals how important we considered the object of our loss.

Depression reveals how important we considered the object of our loss.

5. Acceptance. The healing process nears completion when we can accept the loss. The pain may not have completely subsided, but new hopes and goals do begin to surface. After about a year, grief may peak again. The feelings are intense, but not as long lasting. Remember that this process does not occur in a straight line. We may find ourselves recycling grief that we thought we had resolved.

Life's losses tend to be cumulative. After successfully working through one, we have acquired some background and skills for working through another. The child who loses a valued pet and works through the associated thoughts and feelings gains the experience to face the loss of a more significant relationship—such as a grandparent. Grief feelings, though painful, will not be entirely unfamiliar. Age brings both wisdom and maturity to work through significant losses.

If you are presently experiencing a grief reaction, we encourage you to pray this prayer:

Dear Lord,
I know You understand grief because You experienced the loss of Your Son, Jesus. It must have broken Your heart to send Him to earth to experience shame and death for such an undeserving people. I come to You now asking You to help me accept my losses. Some days are tolerable. Other times it's all I can do to make it through the day. Please bring me to the point of accepting my loss. Intervene in my life right now. Impart Your life to me during this time of loss. Amen.

DAY 2
Hope in the Face of Death

Purpose: To explain the Christian's hope when death occurs

Passage: Read 1 Thessalonians 4:13-18 in preparation for today's study.

Hope in the Resurrection

When someone close to us dies, we experience intense pain followed by a lingering sadness. Scripture acknowledges this experience in its accounts of how Jesus responded to those who mourned.

1. Jesus viewed a funeral procession in Nain and brought a widow's son back to life: "When the Lord saw her, He felt compassion for her" (Luke 7:13).

2. Jesus saw Martha, Mary, and the friends with them grieving and was deeply moved: "Jesus wept. And so the Jews were saying, 'Behold how He loved him!' " (John 11:35-36).

3. Jesus retreated to a lonely place after hearing of the death of John the Baptist. Perhaps He sought comfort from the Father as well as direction: "Now when Jesus heard it, He withdrew … to a lonely place by Himself" (Matt. 14:13).

The Bible responds to the intense grief associated with death by giving us hope in the resurrection of the dead. In other words, we are reminded that our time on earth is only the beginning of a relationship with Christ that will continue beyond death throughout eternity (see John 14:2-3). Yes, Jesus promised that He has gone to prepare a place for us. This hope in life after death has encouraged Christians throughout the centuries.

Jesus promised that He has gone to prepare a place for us.

Consider this scenario: A church leader calls and asks you to accompany him to visit a mutual friend whose Christian grandmother died several weeks ago. He is still having a hard time coping with the loss. How can you use the hope of the resurrection to encourage your friend without sounding uncaring or insensitive? Write your response below.

_____

_____

_____

_____

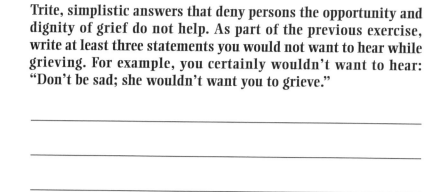

Trite, simplistic answers that deny persons the opportunity and dignity of grief do not help. As part of the previous exercise, write at least three statements you would not want to hear while grieving. For example, you certainly wouldn't want to hear: "Don't be sad; she wouldn't want you to grieve."

_____

_____

_____

We've all heard the words paraphrased from the Hippocratic oath, "first do no harm." The motto certainly applies to those who attempt to care for grieving people. A depressed friend wrote the following words regarding the kind of "help" some well-intended people supply.

> I wish friends would not offer trite, simplistic words. Didn't they know I was reading my Bible and praying! I wanted to please God and be rid of this pain. Why couldn't they see it? How I wish they could see beyond their own lives to mine. At times I felt as if I was in the ocean drowning. It took all I could do to keep my head above water. Along they would come in their fancy ski boat. As they would pass they would shout some new-fangled ideas about staying afloat. What I needed was someone to get in the water with me. How I needed help!

Comfort in the Face of Death

For those who do not know Christ, death is life's greatest tragedy.

For those who do not know Christ, death is life's greatest tragedy. Death is an experience of hopelessness—one from which the deceased and loved ones cannot recover. Although Christians experience intense pain at the loss of a loved one, usually the comfort of Christ and the reality of heaven become even more evident during times of grief.

In 1 Thessalonians 4:13-18, Paul encouraged Christians concerning loved ones who had died.

> But we do not want you to be uninformed, brethren, about those who are asleep, that you may not grieve, as do the rest who have no hope.

Paul wanted believers to have a proper understanding of biblical truth: those fellow believers we lose to death are with the Lord. We will someday join our Christian family members who have gone on before us. If we are still alive when Jesus returns to earth, they will come with Him! "Then we who are alive and remain shall be caught up together with them in the clouds to meet the Lord in the air, and thus we shall always be with the Lord" (1 Thess. 4:17).

As believers, we are never separated from the Lord—in life or in death! This truth explains why our grief is of a different nature from those who do not know Christ. Death has no power over us. Certainly, we suffer pain at the experience of loss, but only because we want to see and be close to those we love. What a blessing to know that we and those we love will always be with the Lord! "Therefore comfort one another with these words" (1 Thess. 4:18).

Remember that the comfort we receive in Christ does not eliminate the grief process you considered in yesterday's study. In response to the Lord's comfort you may sometimes feel disbelief (shock). On another occasion you may feel angry or depressed. Christ's comfort means not so much relief from the pain as strength for the journey.

How do you feel right now about God's comfort in the midst of loss? Circle any responses that describe your feelings, even if those responses don't seem consistent or rational.

angry	sad	grateful	disbelieving
joyful	apathetic	doubtful	mad
tired	happy	other _____	

What are your thoughts about today's Scripture? Has the Lord spoken to you in a personal or significant way about the subject of loss and hope? Express how you feel about the Christian's hope. This is not new information—rather an opportunity to affirm or develop appreciation for what we understand rationally.

_____

_____

_____

_____

_____

DAY 3
Grieving Your Losses

Purpose: To determine how you deal with grief—regardless of the type of loss

Passage: Read Psalm 146 in preparation for today's study.

God offers us hope in the loss of a loved one, but what about times when we lose something else important to us such as a job, home, or relationship? These losses can also result in prolonged sadness and feelings of hopelessness and despair. Certainly these losses can leave a person feeling discouraged and depressed.

Other losses can also result in prolonged sadness and feelings of hopelessness and despair.

Losses You Have Faced

Recall some major losses you have encountered. Facing experiences of loss and moving forward in a positive manner are major parts of personal growth.

Review the list below. Check the losses you have experienced. If we have not included your loss or losses, add them to the list. Beside each you check, indicate how long ago the loss occurred.

❏ job loss
❏ moving away from family and/or friends
❏ loss of an important relationship
❏ miscarriage
❏ expectations
❏ divorce
❏ children leaving home
❏ illness or loss of physical capability
❏ threatened loss such as medical tests or job instability

❏ Other _____

_____

This reflection provides an evaluation of the loss and grieving you have experienced over a specific period of time. As Christians we can learn to face all types of disappointments with hope. Consider Paul's words in Romans 8:28. "We know that God causes all things to work together for good to those who love God, to those who are called according to His purpose." The verse does not promise that all things that happen to us are good. It promises that our God can use the events of our lives to bring His good purpose.

God can use the events of our lives to bring His good purpose.

When we encounter any significant losses, we must be prepared for the accompanying emotions. We must work through the healing process. We cannot suspend and interrupt these normal processes any more than we can suspend the law of gravity or ignore the time necessary for the healing of a broken arm or leg. We can face them confidently and lean on the Lord for strength.

An Example of Loss and Grief

Randy fully expected to retire from his job at Capital City Electric. His supervisors commented on his good work. He received promotions. He never had a hint of poor performance. As far as Randy knew, he had a spotless record. Then after 15 years of loyal service, the company laid him off.

1. *Shock.* When the job-release note appeared on Randy's desk, he was totally surprised. *Surely there's been a mistake,* he thought. Randy immediately went to his supervisor, but there was no mistake: he was now unemployed. He felt numb all over. His mind screamed, *This can't be happening to me!*

"This can't be happening to me!"

2. *Anger.* For the first few days Randy was dazed and troubled. Initially and immediately he decided to trust in the Lord, believing that God had a plan for his life, but eventually anger and bitterness settled in. "I gave them 15 years of hard work and look what they've done to me!" Randy cried. For weeks, similar thoughts consumed Randy's mind. He felt as if he might explode!

3. *What If?* Randy was not only angry but also plagued with constant self-doubt. He continued to ask himself: *What if? What if I had done a better job? Surely they wouldn't have fired me. What if I had arrived at work earlier and left later?* These questions haunted Randy as he analyzed the situation and attempted to regain some control over his life.

Shame vs. Guilt

Continually asking What if? results in false guilt and unrealistic shame. Guilt deals with what you have done while shame focuses on who you are. Of the two, shame has a more negative impact on the one experiencing loss.

The list below includes evidences of shame. Underline the word(s) or phrase(s) you have felt or thought.

1. Believing you are not as good as others

2. Believing you are always wrong or to blame

3. Feeling you are defective

4. The inability to get a mistake you made out of your mind

5. Difficulty forgiving yourself

6. Hesitancy to share your opinion or view

7. Fear that if others really knew you they would reject you

4. *Depression.* The anger Randy felt and his continual reliving of the the situation resulted in sadness and a pattern of self-condemnation. Counselors define this as "anger turned inward." Randy believed he was the problem and turned his angry feelings against himself. He was also sad because his career took an unexpected turn.

5. *Acceptance.* After several months, Randy began to experience hope. The pain remained to a certain extent, but he began to set some goals. He no longer viewed himself as responsible for his job loss. He recognized that his job loss resulted from a major company downsizing. Randy resolved the matter and reached a healthy acceptance of the circumstances.

Psalm 146 admonishes us to place our hope in the Lord for blessing rather than trusting in powerful men (princes) in whom we can find no salvation. Randy knew this truth, but as he worked through his grief, passages like Psalm 146 took on a new meaning for him. In fact, he later found a job that employed his skills more extensively and brought new challenges into his life. He shared what he had learned in a men's group at church, commenting with newfound enthusiasm on the work God had accomplished in his life.

How blessed is he whose help is the God of Jacob,
Whose hope is in the Lord his God (Ps. 146:5).

Randy's continual reliving of the situation resulted in sadness and a pattern of self-condemnation.

Your Experience with the Stages of Grief

To some extent we have all experienced the stages of grief. Complete the following scale to determine which of the stages you have encountered most often. Choose a specific loss in your life. By each stage mark the appropriate number corresponding with your experience. (You might work through this chart with several different losses to see how you responded to each.)

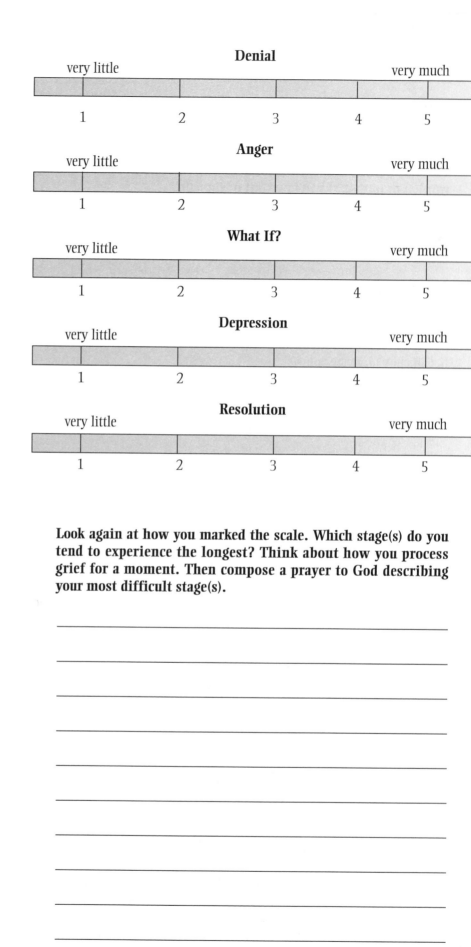

Denial

very little · · · · · very much

1 2 3 4 5

Anger

very little · · · · · very much

1 2 3 4 5

What If?

very little · · · · · very much

1 2 3 4 5

Depression

very little · · · · · very much

1 2 3 4 5

Resolution

very little · · · · · very much

1 2 3 4 5

Look again at how you marked the scale. Which stage(s) do you tend to experience the longest? Think about how you process grief for a moment. Then compose a prayer to God describing your most difficult stage(s).

_____

_____

_____

_____

_____

_____

_____

_____

DAY 4
Moving Beyond Your Losses

Purpose: To cope with a loss by establishing new goals

Passage: Read Jeremiah 29:11 in preparation for today's study.

Previously we learned that when a person fully accepts a loss, the pain is not necessarily gone, but new hopes and goals emerge. Today's study focuses on the three key components of the "acceptance" stage of grieving. They include:
- believing God has plans for your future;
- being willing to make a life for yourself; and
- setting new goals.

Believing God Has Plans for Your Future

> "For I know the plans that I have for you," declares the Lord, "plans for welfare and not for calamity to give you a future and a hope" (Jer. 29:11).

God told Jeremiah to write to the exiles in Babylon. He was to tell them that, while the exile would last 70 years, the Lord had not forgotten them. Though they were far from their home, they were not to abandon hope and lose sight of God's care.

Every aspect of the Christian life involves faith. We need faith to recognize not only that God exists but also that He loves us and is intimately involved in our lives. Experiences of loss challenge this belief. We wonder, *How could a loving Heavenly Father allow this to happen to me?* The answer does not come easily, but acceptance of a loss involves believing God has a special plan for your future: "Plans for welfare and not for calamity to give you a future and a hope."

Acceptance of a loss involves believing God has a special plan for your future.

God has plans for your life that include a future and hope. Great news! However, during periods of deep discouragement, believing is difficult because life seems so bleak and dark. Below list any words you think describe your future right now.

Choosing God's plan for you will require you to trust in Him, not yourself. Trusting is neither easy nor simple. Begin by asking God to place in your heart His hope for a meaningful future. Take time to express your prayer to Him right now.

Being Willing to Make a Life for Yourself

Acceptance means being willing to accept life as it is rather than how we might like it to be. It also means making a decision to move beyond what was lost to embrace what lies ahead. The key word is *willingness*.

Be strong, and let your heart take courage,
All you who hope in [or wait for] the Lord (Ps. 31:24).

Often willingness is a matter of strength and courage. In Psalm 31 David spoke to those who are most able to be courageous—those who have placed their hope in the Lord. Embracing what lies ahead involves taking responsibility for your future. It includes utilizing the strength God supplies to do those things that will accomplish His good plan for you. A helpful motto is: This is my life and with God's help I will make something out of it that glorifies Him.

Would you be willing to take responsibility for your part in growing through loss? It may require courage you believe you do not possess. The following covenant clarifies your commitment to our Heavenly Father.

This is my life and with God's help I will make something out of it that glorifies Him.

Responsibility Covenant

Father, I realize I cannot passively sit by and do nothing about coping with loss. Yet, I am not sure of the next step. I covenant with You to be responsible by daily believing You. Before I get out of bed each day I will begin by praying: Lord, this is Your day and I give it completely to You. Take charge of all that I think, say, and do. Also, I will intercede for at least one friend each day, asking you to strengthen him or her. I agree to do these things as You accomplish Your work in me. Amen.

Setting New Goals

We have considered two key components: belief and willingness. Now, let's look at the third aspect of acceptance—goal-setting.

Goals represent specific plans we intend to accomplish. Randy lost a job he enjoyed but eventually was able to set a new goal: to obtain a position that utilized more of his abilities and skills. When Susan's fiancé died, she was devastated. With the help of family and friends, she worked through the difficult grief process to confront feelings of sadness, anger, and frustration.

One year after the death of Susan's fiancé, she still experienced painful feelings, but she began to understand that God really was involved in her life—He wanted the best for her and had planned a special future just for her. With new-found hope, she returned to college and graduated in three years.

Several college administrators recognized Susan's maturity and asked her to serve as her dormitory's student advisor during her senior year. This experience revealed skills she had not previously considered. Now she is preparing to enter graduate school with a goal to become a counselor. When Susan reflected on the past four years, she recognized that God had strengthened her. His plans certainly were "for welfare and not for calamity to give [her] a future and a hope."

When setting goals for ourselves or helping others to do so, remember to follow these three guidelines. Make goals:

Susan recognized that God had strengthened her.

1. *brief enough to be remembered.* Is the goal simple enough that I can discuss it with a friend without referring to written plans?
2. *specific enough to be written down.* Can I describe it in one sentence?
3. *clear enough to be achieved.* Will I know when I've attained the goal? For example, we set a goal three years ago and were able to buy a house last month.

For the goal to be clear, it must be measurable. Clear, measurable goals look like this: (a) I will pray daily for those I know who have experienced a recent loss; (b) Each day I will journal my feelings about the loss.

Setting realistic goals is one way to create hope while coping with loss. Share your goals with a friend to establish an accountability partner.

Brief, specific, and clear are the three key descriptors of effective goal-setting. Using those ingredients, try your hand at establishing one goal for yourself. Write it in the space below.

_____

_____

_____

Now re-read your goal. Does it contain each effective goal-setting ingredient? Was the goal:

     ___ brief?   ___specific?   ___ clear?

DAY 5
Helping Others

Purpose: To discover ways we can minister to those who are grieving

Passage: Read Isaiah 61:1-3 in preparation for today's study.

Looking Back at Days 1-4

In the past four days we have studied the pattern of grieving significant losses. Here's a brief review:

- Day 1: The normal grief process is God's way of helping us to resolve our losses. For most people, grief follows a fairly predictable pattern including five stages.
- Day 2: The Bible offers comfort for the intense grief associated with death by giving us hope in the resurrection of the dead. Christians face intense pain at the loss of a loved one, but death has no victory over believers. We and those we love will always be close to the Lord!
- Day 3: What about the times we lose something else important to us such as a job, a home, or a relationship? These loss experiences also follow a normal grief process which leads to healing and acceptance.
- Day 4: The Bible assures us that God plans to give us a future and a hope. We move beyond our losses by accepting this truth with a willingness to make a life for ourselves and to set new goals.

Today we will focus on ways we can minister to others who are experiencing the pain of losing someone or something of value.

How Can We Minister to Those Who Grieve?

What are some things we can do for others as they grieve? The following suggestions, although simple, are priceless in the lives of those we love.

Immediately After the Loss

Approaching a grieving person becomes increasingly awkward if you delay.

1. *Make contact as soon as possible.* Reach out to the hurting one either in person, by phone, or by card. Approaching a grieving person becomes increasingly awkward if you delay. **Remember:** grief enjoys company!

2. *Be specific in your offers to help.* Avoid saying, "Call me if I can help." Death and other losses are often crisis situations, so people both need and appreciate relief. Below are some specific ways to help:
   a. Offer transportation to and from the airport.
   b. House out-of-town relatives or friends, possibly offering a car.
   c. Provide meals (for example, send chili for a large gathering of extended family members).
   d. Offer to do house cleaning or laundry before company arrives, a big relief to one who is overwhelmed.
   e. Cut the grass and do other yard work.
   f. Offer a few specific times you can baby-sit if needed.
   g. Answer the phone during a specified period of time.
   h. Inquire about funeral plans.
As a rule of thumb, if you think of something that would help you, it probably would be helpful to someone else.

Remember that the person needs to talk about it.

3. *Allow the grieving person to talk and prepare to listen.* Remember that the person who lost something or someone needs to talk about it. For the grieving person to share the details of the loss repeatedly is not unusual. This helps him or her to process and come to terms with the loss.

4. *Tell the grieving person that it's OK to need others.* Listening, perhaps the greatest gift, includes time, attention, and a desire to understand. Avoid telling a person what to do. Explain that postponing major decisions is often best. **Remember:** be faithful. To commit to a little and be faithful is better than to commit to that which you cannot accomplish.

After Time Has Passed

1. *Send a card.* Share some personal story or characteristic you remember about the one who died. Remember: death does not terminate a relationship; it changes it. Surviving family members want to keep the memories alive.

2. *Pay special attention to holidays.* They can be lonely. Offer understanding and communicate that it's OK to talk about happy memories. This is helpful to the grieving person.

What Can We Say to Those Who Are Grieving?

The following lists contains examples of expressions to use or to avoid in dealing with someone who has suffered a loss. Consider using the statements that help the next time you deal with a grieving person.

Statements That Hinder the Healing Process	Statements That Help the Healing Process
Time will heal.	This pain must feel as though it will go on forever.
Look at the bright side.	The day must seem so dark.
All Christians suffer.	This suffering must seem unbearable.
With faith you can escape the pain.	This hurts. I'm glad Jesus listens to us.
You must be strong.	You don't need to be strong for me.
You need to stay faithful to God.	We need to pray that God would comfort you in this difficult time.
You probably want to be alone.	Let me come over so we can talk.
God has a plan.	This must seem to make no sense at all. In time maybe we will understand God's plan more fully.
I know just how you feel!	I know I don't understand how you feel.
Just put it aside in your mind.	Believe it or not, talking really does help.
Don't be sad. He/she is with God.	It must seem lonely without him/her.

[1] *Webster's Ninth Collegiate Dictionary*, ed. Frederick C. Mish, (Springfield: Merriam-Webster Inc., 1991), 537.

Week 4

Loss: The Place I Called Home

Case in Point

Why did Dad do it? This question continued to race through Kevin's mind. No matter how he tried to distract himself, the question persisted.

At the age of 21, Kevin sat in his pastor's office pouring out the pain caused by his alcoholic father. The pastor listened as Kevin revealed how his father had physically and verbally abused his mother and all three children. Certainly Kevin's family wasn't what he wished it had been: a place of love and support. He knew he had missed something vital while growing up, and the hurt his dad caused now permeated Kevin's thoughts, feelings, and actions. The pastor pondered how he might help this depressed young man.

Those wounded by their families and those desiring to help the wounded can benefit by understanding family loss—the reality that our family did not meet our needs. This week's study will help us to understand the impact of family pain on people like Kevin and the avenues that lead to healing, change, and growth.

This week you will...
- identify characteristics of healthy families;
- recognize some causes of family dysfunction;
- examine how one Bible character dealt with family of origin pain;
- learn how past family pain contributes to depression;
- implement strategies that motivate recovery.

What you will study
Day 1: What Is a Healthy Family?
Day 2: What Happened to the Family?
Day 3: Hezekiah's Damaged Dad
Day 4: Family Pain and Adult Depression
Day 5: Hope from a Painful Childhood

Memory verse
"He will restore the hearts of the fathers to their children, and the hearts of the children to their fathers" (Mal. 4:6).

DAY 1
What Is a Healthy Family?

Purpose: To explain the differences between healthy and unhealthy families

Passage: Read Deuteronomy 6:5-9 in preparation for today's study.

None of us grew up in perfectly healthy families. Thus, all of us experience some painful memories. For some people, however, family pain is a source of discouragement and depression. The pain some families feel resides in the past, but many people also experience on-going hurt in the area of family life.

An unhealthy family environment creates major losses, and every major loss needs to be grieved. Perhaps you have struggled with the discrepancy between the reality of your family of origin and what you wish it had been. This week's study will help you to understand that God uses the grief process as a way for you to resolve your losses.

Don't you wish that family problems, like the common cold, had clear symptoms which are easily identified and treated? It would be great if all families were free from symptoms of dysfunction, but when sin entered the world it marred everything, including families. Remember—when we refer to healthy families in today's study, we mean better-functioning families, not perfect ones. You will only find perfect families in heaven!

Let's see what the Bible says about healthy families.

God's Design for Healthy Families

Deuteronomy 6 contains some clear directives for strong, godly families that provide a starting point for our study.

Healthy families need a solid foundation built on the love of God.

1. *Love the Lord with all your heart* (v. 5). Moses spoke to the families of Israel and reminded them to love the Lord supremely. God was to be the object of their love. Today God intends for our homes to radiate love for Him and for our relationship with Him to be more important than work, hobbies, money, or anything else. Healthy families need a solid foundation built on the love of God.

2. *Imbed God's Word on your heart* (v. 6). The commitment the Israelites had to God and His Word was to be more than mere external ritual. The Word of God was to be imbedded in the hearts of parents. When we were children, God desired that our parents model to us a deep personal closeness with the Savior. He intended for us to consistently see, hear, and experience our parents' love for God.

3. *Teach your children to love God and His Word* (vv. 7-9). Parenting must be intentional. Parents must make a concerted effort to communicate to children their relationship to God and love for His Word. Healthy parents seek to instill a love for God in their children. Deuteronomy 6:7-9 explains how and when God's Word should be taught: "You shall teach them diligently to your sons and shall talk of them when you sit in your house and when you walk by the way and when you lie down and when you rise up."

So when and where should God's Word be taught? Everywhere and all the time. A parent's love for God should be a daily, consistent lifestyle. "You shall bind them as a sign on your hand and they shall be as frontals on your forehead" (v. 8).

How important is God's Word to parenting? Parents need to place God's Word at the center of their actions and thoughts. "You shall write them on the doorposts of your house and on your gates" (v. 9).

Where does the Bible command parents to keep God's Word? "On the doorposts" indicates that parents were to have God's Word in their hearts as they entered their houses and as they went out into their communities. "On your gates" indicates God's Word working to influence local government, since "gates" in Old Testament times referred to the seat of local government.

As you grew up, how many of the principles in Deuteronomy 6 were present in your family? Circle the phrase that describes how frequently your parents displayed the following qualities.

Love the Lord with all your heart.

none	some	most of the time	consistently

These words ... shall be on your heart.

none	some	most of the time	consistently

You shall teach them diligently to your children.

none	some	most of the time	consistently

Characteristics of Healthy Families

God made families to be unique. For example, one family may be socially active, while another enjoys a more quiet lifestyle, but positive general characteristics apply to all family types. Let's examine some major indicators of family health.

1. *In a healthy family, parents have an intimate marriage.* A healthy, intimate marriage is foundational to effective parenting. Mom and Dad obviously love each other. They enjoy each other's presence and company. They spend time building their relationship with God and each other. Each spouse has learned to balance outside demands with marital responsibilities.

Place an X on the spot that most closely reflects the degree this characteristic was present in your family of origin.

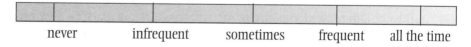

never	infrequent	sometimes	frequent	all the time

2. *A healthy family permits you to be yourself and accepts you as such.* Healthy families value closeness. They enjoy being a family but at the same time allow

each member to be him- or herself. For instance, as parents we might like our children to be involved with sports because we enjoy them, but if our children decide to join the concert band or choir, we should be their biggest cheerleaders. We don't try to live our lives through our children.

On the scale below place an X on the spot that reflects this characteristic in your family of origin.

never	infrequent	sometimes	frequent	all the time

3. *Healthy families practice open communication.* Healthy families discuss a variety of topics. The husband and wife place a high priority on sharing with each other. An intimate marriage requires that both spouses put forth the effort to communicate. Parents understand that children and adults communicate differently. Children require more patience, understanding, and time.

Healthy families permit members to both feel and express feelings. Parents seek to encourage their children to identify and share emotions, ignoring the old saying, "Children are to be seen and not heard" and modeling healthy expression of emotions. They also teach children to share honestly their emotions with the Heavenly Father.

Healthy families permit members to both feel and express feelings.

On the scale below, place an X on the spot that reflects this characteristic in your family of origin.

never	infrequent	sometimes	frequent	all the time

4. *Healthy families share encouragement and affirmation.* An older gentleman once said, "It takes a whole lot of encouragement to hurt a person." In other words, you really can't hurt folks by encouraging them too much! Unfortunately, some parents believe this approach makes children soft or vain. This world can be a discouraging place, so we all need affirmation.

When a husband and wife encourage each other with actions and words, the children imitate this pattern. In a healthy home, family members build up one another. Statements like these are frequent:

"Son, you did a great job!"
"I am so glad God gave you to me!"
"Hang in there! I know you can do it!"
"I'm praying for you!"
"You sure make that dress look beautiful!"

"It takes a whole lot of encouragement to hurt a person."

Can you recall encouraging statements your parents made to you? List them below.

_____

_____

_____

_____

If you are unable to remember encouraging statements from your parents, list statements you wish you had heard.

_____

_____

_____

On the scale below, place an X on the spot that reflects this characteristic in your family of origin.

never	infrequent	sometimes	frequent	all the time

A healthy family teaches members to take their cares and problems to the Heavenly Father.

5. _A healthy family makes home a safe place._ Members feel accepted. They learn from experience that the family will be consistently supportive. Members feel safe to share fears and doubts. The family does not perpetuate unrealistic shame and blame. A healthy family teaches members to take their cares and problems to their Heavenly Father. They learn to trust the Heavenly Father because earthly family members are trustworthy.

Place an X on the area that best reflects this characteristic in your family of origin.

never	infrequent	sometimes	frequent	all the time

6. _Healthy families view conflict as a part of normal family life._ Healthy families acknowledge that differences lead to disagreement. They use conflicts in a positive way to deepen intimacy between family members and God by working through problems. Because love is the family theme, disagreement rarely leaves a person shamed, isolated, or abandoned. Consequently, each member of the family learns to discover hope, even in difficult times.

Place an X on the block that reflects this characteristic in your family of origin.

never	infrequent	sometimes	frequent	all the time

Take a moment and talk to our Lord about the family in which you grew up. Share with Him the joy or pain you experienced. Invite Him to help and heal. Record your thoughts and feelings.

_____

_____

_____

_____

DAY 2
What Happened to the Family?

Purpose: To identify how sin impacts the family

Passage: Read Genesis 3 in preparation for today's study.

Sometimes nursery rhymes express ideas more clearly than adult explanations. Consider Humpty Dumpty. The lines of verse describe the condition of many present-day families.

> *Humpty Dumpty sat on a wall.*
> *Humpty Dumpty had a great fall.*
> *All the king's horses and all the king's men*
> *Couldn't put Humpty together again.*

The family had a great fall.
- the brokenness of divorce
- the scars of abuse
- the difficulties of single-parent families
- the workaholic parent
- the addicted family member
- the busyness of daily chores

All the king's horses and all the king's men can't put the family together again. The family desperately needs help. The following examples indicate those seeking to be knights in shining armor, working to save the family.
- therapists
- new medications
- seminars
- books geared to family needs, types, communication, and more
- audio- and videotapes
- pastors and teachers

"Lord, designer of family and family life, we desperately need you!"

> *Dear Lord,*
> *You are the designer of family and family life. We desperately need You! Our families hurt so badly. We truly are like "sheep with no shepherd." Shepherd us, Lord. How we need You! We cry out to you amidst our pain and hurt, knowing that You hold the answers to family needs. Forgive us for being slow to turn to You for help. Heal us we pray. Amen.*

The Beginning of Family Problems

Chapter 2 of Genesis portrays a wonderful picture of intimacy between Adam and Eve in the garden of Eden. This closeness was the direct result of their profound intimacy with God and was part of His wise design.

However, in chapter 3, we see this oneness shattered like a precious piece of china hurled against the floor—forever broken. The difference between the broken piece of china and broken humanity is that we have a Redeemer, Jesus Christ. He longs to reestablish oneness with us (see John 17:20-23). Yes, God provides hope for broken, hurting families! That hope is found in Jesus Christ's love for you!

Satan's Scheme

God provides hope in the person of Jesus Christ for broken, hurting families!

Satan approached Eve indirectly, then directly. In Genesis 3:1 he questioned God's words. The enemy's words were penetrating, as if to ask, "Did God *really* say…?" His plan was to plant a seed of doubt. Then Satan directly approached Eve by calling God a liar. That's right, Satan called God a liar! Look at the verses for yourself. "You surely shall not die. For God knows that in the day you eat from it your eyes will be opened, and you will be like God, knowing good and evil" (Gen. 3:4-5).

Notice that Satan did not attack Adam and Eve's marriage. Instead he attacked God's reliability. He raised several questions for these two vulnerable humans.

1. Is God trustworthy?
2. Does God have your best interest in mind?
3. Is God holding back something good from you?
4. Is God really who you think He is?

The enemy laid his trap well and ensnared the human race. He achieved his goal; he destroyed intimacy between Adam and Eve and between humans and God.

The Consequences of Adam and Eve's Sin

Sin has consequences, some immediate and some delayed, but sin always demands a price. Look at the results of Adam's and Eve's sin.

1. *Adam and Eve avoided God after eating the forbidden fruit* (v. 7). For the first time in their lives they were afraid of the Creator who walked with them in the cool of the day (vv. 8-10). Consequently, men and women have become good at hiding from God and one another.

2. *When God confronted Adam, Adam blamed Eve* (vv. 11-12). Although Adam loved his wife, his sin led to a tremendous sense of self-protection. Adam's main goal became: "Take care of myself at all costs!" His self-protection caused him to turn his back on his life companion. Eve, not to be outdone, passed the buck to the serpent (v. 13). Much family strife results from attacking and blaming.

3. *Adam and Eve's sin damaged their children* (Gen. 4:8). Genesis, chapter 4 introduces us to the children of Adam and Eve. After only one generation, the first murder occurred. Cain murdered Abel, his brother.

Family Problems Today

Families today face problems similar to those described in the first few chapters of Genesis. We also fall victim to Satan's lies about our Father. Mates and children continue to avoid and attack, and, all too often children carry the scars of self-protective parents.

Did the family you grew up in avoid confronting problems directly? ❏ yes ❏ no **If so, give an example of how family members avoided problems.**

_____

Did family members blame others, especially other family members? ❏ yes ❏ no **If so, give an example.**

_____

If you are or are planning to be a parent, what is one thing you want to change between how you relate to your children and how your parents related to you?

_____

Cracks in Today's Family

The family today suffers from an amazing array of compulsive behaviors. All these patterns take a huge toll on the emotional resources needed to function as family members.

Look at the following list of issues families face today. Circle the ones you experienced in childhood.

Busyness	Workaholism	Perfectionism
Materialism	Applying Guilt	Applying Blame
Neglect	Physical Abuse	Verbal Abuse
Sexual Abuse	Divorce	Single-Parent Family

Did you circle at least one of these? Identifying what you experienced may be painful, but it is the first step toward change. When you are objective about the past, you begin to see the present results of past experience.

These issues are definitely unsettling. God desires for all families to be healthy. However, even if today your immediate family is healthy, you may be hurting as a result of growing up in a family that did not know positive ways to express love and care for you. Many parents were damaged by the parenting they experienced. Hope comes from recognizing the damage and turning to God and others for help.

Remember—the healing process is a journey.

Today's study and work may have been intense for you. Take a few minutes to process this material with your Heavenly Father. Go for a prayerwalk. Tell Christ your feelings about your childhood. You may need to ask His help in dealing with those feelings. Remember this process is a journey.

DAY 3
Hezekiah's Damaged Dad

Purpose: To examine how one Bible character handled family loss

Passage: Read 2 Kings 16:1-20 in preparation for today's study.

"I'm a Christian now. Why do I still have these problems with my dad?" Eric asked. He was feeling both angry and frustrated as he spoke these words to his Sunday School teacher. Mr. Johnson smiled and said gently, "It would be great, wouldn't it, if all our past problems were immediately erased when we entered into a relationship with Christ?"

The teacher knew Eric faced tremendous personal pain as a result of his dad's raging episodes. He put his hand on Eric's shoulder and assured him that God wants to strengthen, guide, and comfort him in dealing with this pain. Mr. Johnson also assured Eric that he would be available.

Eric is not alone when it comes to children hurt by their parents. Today, let's look at an Old Testament king who overcame the influence of a damaging dad.

A Look at a Dysfunctional Dad

When considering sources of help, God should be the One to whom we turn first.

1. *Ahaz did not do right.* Second Kings 16:1-20 provides us with a clear picture of Ahaz, the father of Hezekiah. Verse 2 records these words: "[Ahaz] did not do what was right in the sight of the Lord his God, as his father David had done."

Ahaz ignored God and the godly example provided for him in King David. Instead, he chose to follow Israel's disobedient kings. Like Ahaz, many of our parents followed and left bad examples.

Ahaz burned incense and sacrificed at least one of his own children to a false deity (vv. 3-4). Most of us cannot even imagine the cruel behavior and influence to which Hezekiah was subjected.

2. *Ahaz did not rely on God* (vv. 7-10). When Ahaz encountered trouble, he turned to the king of Assyria. Instead of crying out to God for help, he chose a human aid. He did not even consider God as a source of help in times of need. We are not suggesting that a person should refuse help from others. What we are saying is that God should be the One to whom we turn first. Ahaz stooped so low as to use the gold and silver from the Lord's house to buy the protection of the king of Assyria (vv. 8-9). Ahaz was definitely a poor example for young Hezekiah.

How would you describe your parents' relationship to God? Write your response below.

_____

_____

_____

_____

Hezekiah Overcomes His Painful Past

Hezekiah made several choices that helped him to overcome many of the effects of his painful past.

1. *He selected a good role model* (2 Kings18: 3). The Bible says Hezekiah "did right in the sight of the Lord, according to all that his father David had done." If you did not have a positive role model in your immediate family—look elsewhere! It may take a little time and work, but the benefits are worth it. Ask God to lead you to one who will help you overcome your past by setting a good example.

Ask God to lead you to one who will help you overcome your past by setting a good example.

2. *He removed distractions* (v. 4). Hezekiah removed all influences of his father's false worship. In the same way, before you can effectively rebuild, you may have to tear down some ideas and habits that were constructed in your past. Do you carry any of the following with you?

- the belief that you must be perfect to be loved
- the belief that the family's problems are your fault
- addictive and self-destructive behavior
- extreme avoidance of people
- anger and criticism of others

The list could go on. But let's take a moment to consider your past family and the negative "constructions" you may need to tear down.

Complete the following sentence in the space provided below. "The most common problem(s) I had with my parents was…" (Perhaps the following examples will help you get started):

1. I could never live up to their expectations.
2. They did not listen to me.
3. We fought all the time.
4. They were so busy they had little time for me.

_____

_____

What past learned behaviors can you begin to change today?

_____

What patterns can you address in the future?

_____

3. *He relied on God* (vv. 5-6). Hezekiah trusted God, a completely opposite behavior than what his father practiced. God provided Hezekiah as an example of one who overcame the influence of a damaging parent. If you did not grow up with godly parents, then God wants you to begin passing the baton of faith. Our children and grandchildren can inherit a stronger foundation because we trusted God.

If you did not grow up with godly parents, then God wants you to begin passing the baton of faith to your children.

What type of influence would you like to have on those closest to you? Complete this sentence: When I die I would like those closest to me to describe my impact on their lives with these words:

_____

_____

We encourage you to pray the following prayer:

Lord,
May those who follow me find me faithful. May the life I have lived provide direction for my spouse, children, grandchildren, and friends. May the footprints I leave behind lead them to faith in Christ; may my life inspire them to obey and love You. Thank You for true hope in Jesus Christ. Amen.

DAY 4
Family Pain and Adult Depression

Purpose: To identify present indicators of past family pain

Passage: Read Proverbs 13:13-16 in preparation for today's study.

When we were born our parents received an assignment from God—to introduce us to His grace. They were to communicate this grace through an intimate relationship with them. Some of our parents successfully accomplished this task, others did not. Either way, they had tremendous impact on who we are today.

Ignoring the Past

In a counseling situation, we sometimes use a simple illustration to relate to the danger caused by ignoring the past. You purchase a car, but when you arrive home one of the lug nuts is missing from the left front wheel. It doesn't appear to be an urgent problem so you ignore it. After all, someone else did the work, so why should you worry about it? Two days later you notice that another nut has vibrated loose and is missing. Once again you pay no attention because you already lost the nut. It's over. Why worry about something in the past? Unfortunately, a week later your tire comes off while driving down the interstate. You hit another vehicle before colliding with a tree. Both your car and the one you hit are totaled. Suddenly the past problem (loose and missing lug nuts) has directly impacted your present. Ignoring the influence of the past has contributed to the present damages.

Ignoring the influence of the past contributes to present damages.

Consider the following parallels between how the past influences the present:

1. We did not have a choice about some past problems.

It's not my fault that I bought a car with a missing lug nut.

2. We must recognize the impact of the past and be willing to repair the damage.

It's my responsibility to replace the missing lug nut.

3. We will experience more hurt and pain if we ignore the past.

Ignoring the missing lug nuts led to compounded problems.

How much has the past influenced your present life in a negative fashion? <u>Circle</u> <u>the</u> word that best represents the amount of past influence.

none	a little	some	much	too much

We must recognize the impact of the past and be willing to repair the damage.

Present Indicators of Past Family Pain

The following patterns represent warning signals. When we see them, God is showing us that a lug nut is loose or missing. They alert us to consider ways past family pain is affecting our present-day living.

1. *Irrational Thoughts.* Nagging thought patterns often reveal past pain.

Place a check mark by those thoughts most common to you.

❑ Others' feelings are more important than my own.
❑ I am worthless and unlovable.
❑ Bad love is better than no love at all.
❑ If people I care about reject me, I must be unlovable.
❑ I must be dependent on others or I won't survive.
❑ If I am good I will be loved.
❑ I am responsible for the behavior and feelings of others.
❑ I am responsible for making others change.
❑ I cannot trust anyone but myself.
❑ I am bad if I feel angry.
❑ I must keep peace at all costs.
❑ I can never change.
❑ I can never make mistakes.

Which of the above thoughts is most troublesome to you? Put a star beside it. Below explain how your past produced that thought pattern.

_____

_____

_____

_____

2. *Extreme Busyness.* America has been diagnosed with "hurry up" sickness. It seems we have adopted the belief that "quicker is better." At times, fast-paced living serves as a distraction or anesthetic for those suffering from past pain. Many who have experienced family loss develop the motto: "If I can just stay busy enough, I will no longer hurt."

3. *Acceptance and Approval Hunger.* All of us have a normal need for acceptance, but those who grew up in a dysfunctional family often possess an insatiable appetite for acceptance. Their central focus in life is to earn affirmation—no matter what the cost. They push themselves beyond reasonable limits and compromise their values in the pursuit of approval. Many try to meet the need for acceptance with a career or a relationship.

4. *Hopelessness or Despair.* "It's just no use. Nothing ever works!" Perhaps you've said these words or heard someone else say them. Hopelessness is common among those who have experienced past family pain. A gnawing sense of despair accompanies the thought that they can never gratify their inner hunger for hope and peace. It's a cycle: they experience a few positive and hopeful days followed by several discouraging days.

5. *Difficulty Trusting Others.* Close relationships seem impossible to achieve; attempts to develop deep friendships constantly fail. Non-trusting people tend to develop one or more of the following three relationship styles:
   a. Hide from you style: this person intentionally avoids people. His or her basic belief is: "If I stay away from people, they can't hurt me."
   b. Hurt you style: this individual is overly aggressive. His or her basic belief is: "If I dominate people, they will never hurt me."
   c. Hug you style: this person seeks to please others at all costs. His or her basic belief is this: "If I am nice enough to people, they will not hurt me."

A better alternative to these three relationship styles exists. We call it vulnerable intimacy. Genuine intimacy minimizes defensive protective maneuvers and maximizes transparency.

Genuine intimacy minimizes defensive protective maneuvers and maximizes transparency.

Which of the three relationship styles do you use most often?

_____

Which of the styles do you practice occasionally?

_____

How would you have to change to develop open and transparent relationships? Write your response below.

_____

_____

_____

_____

6. *Distorted View of God.* Many people view God as distant, angry, harsh, uncaring, or insensitive. We may be afraid of God and live in a state of constant anxiety. We may even completely give up on God, believing we can never please Him. Among all these variables, one fact remains constant—parents and significant others can distort an accurate view of the Heavenly Father.

These indicators are caution lights to warn adults of impending danger. If these issues go unaddressed, they may result in deep discouragement or serious depression. Identifying them now and working on them leads to hope.

Parents and significant others can distort an accurate view of the Heavenly Father.

Evaluate how often you experience each of the indicators we have considered today. Beside each of the examples below, write an F for frequently, an O for occasionally, or an S for seldom.

___ irrational thoughts

___ extreme busyness

___ acceptance and approval hunger

___ hopelessness or despair

___ difficulty trusting others

___ distorted view of God

What can you do today to begin working on the indicator(s) you experience frequently or occasionally? Write your response below.

_____

_____

_____

Take a moment and talk to God concerning the indicators. Tell God how you feel about your present situation. Ask Him to show you how to begin recovering from your family pain.

DAY 5
Hope from a Painful Childhood

Purpose: To develop a plan to remedy childhood loss

Passage: Read Hebrews 13:5 in preparation for today's study.

This week we have taken a close look at the way families work. Perhaps you are surprised at what you learned about your family of origin. Let's review what we have learned.

1. Healthy families are identified by their intimacy between family members and with God. As a matter of fact, this relationship is a distinctive of spiritually mature families.

2. Sin damaged intimacy with God and intimacy in marriage. It even impacted the way our children relate to one another.

3. Hezekiah serves as an example of how to work through problems created by a damaging parent.

4. Examples of how past pain may be affecting our lives today demonstrate how childhood hurts become adult injuries.

God truly wants to help you with your pain and difficulties.

Today's study offers a plan everyone can use to deal with destructive patterns in his or her life. God truly wants to help you with your pain and difficulties. So let's get started.

Things to Remember

You are not alone. As you are working through painful issues of loss you may think no one else has ever been through an experience like yours. The loneliness and sense of abandonment can feel suffocating.

Many times we resurrect painful feelings from our past and experience them in the present. Two things will see us through. First, we need to remember that God will never leave us. He is not like damaging parents. As Hebrews 13:5 reminds us, God promises, " 'I will never leave you nor forsake you' " (NKJV).

Locate and read these passages in your Bible. They talk about God's abiding presence. Jot down the main idea of each.

Exodus 3:7-10 _____

John 14:15-18 _____

Romans 8:15-17 _____

Isaiah 41:10 _____

God not only promises His presence, but He also provides others to walk with you through the dark valley.

God not only promises His presence, but He also provides others to walk with you through the dark valley. To ask others to help you during this time is OK. Allow others to know of the burden you carry; they will share the load.

Healing is a process. We said in week 3 that every major loss needs to be grieved. The lack of a healthy family represents a true and major loss. For many of us, the damage we sustained occurred over many years. So it makes sense that the healing process will take time. We often have great difficulty seeing the necessity of the healing process because we want the pain, hurt, and confusion over now! We need to understand and accept the key fact that God loves us no matter how troubled we feel. Romans 8:38-39 states this truth clearly: "I am persuaded, that neither death, nor life, nor angels, nor principalities, nor powers, nor things present, nor things to come, nor height, nor depth, nor any other creature, shall be able to separate us from the love of God, which is in Christ Jesus our Lord" (KJV).

Things to Do

Forgiveness is more than a simple decision. Forgiving is a process.

So what must we do to overcome childhood pain through abuse or neglect? We need to work at the following five practical steps:

1. *Forgive.* When others hurt us, we need to forgive. Forgiveness frees us from the other person's control. When we forgive, we do not let the other person off the hook. When we forgive, we unchain ourselves, but forgiveness is more than a simple decision. Forgiving is a process.

Before you can forgive you must be willing to honestly admit to the hurt others have caused you. Denying your pain will only continue the pain. Ask God to make you fully aware of how badly you hurt and empower you to forgive as He has forgiven you. The process of forgiveness starts with your choice to forgive. Then you must continue to forgive when anger, bitterness, and resentment arise within you. Do not be surprised when you have bad feelings toward the one who hurt you even after you have genuinely forgiven him or her. Simply continue forgiving. Choose not to engage in unforgiveness.

Below list people who hurt you and how they hurt you. Fill in the date when you choose to forgive them.

Person's Name	**Hurt He or She Caused**	**Forgiving Date**

Do you feel that forgiveness involves more than you have yet been able to muster? Remember that genuine forgiveness is a process. We will deal more deeply with forgiveness in week 8.

2. *Lower your expectations.* Not knowing how to set realistic standards and goals can be the result of growing up in a damaged family. We may have a tendency to think that we can do more than can possibly be done. Sometimes we fear we are doomed to distort expectations for the rest of our lives. We can take positive steps to develop realistic expectations. Write out a daily "to do" list, then remove two or three items. The results make life more manageable.

3. *Seek out help.* When you are hurting and feeling abandoned is not the time to be a hero and attempt to handle your problems alone. God created us for fellowship with Himself and others. He never intended for us to be a "Lone Ranger." He intends for us to get support from the family of God. Let us caution you that not every member of the body of Christ will understand what you are going through. Don't stop seeking help and support just because some do not understand. Also, don't be afraid to seek professional help if necessary.

God never intended for you to be a "Lone Ranger."

4. *Replace achieving with receiving.* Many of us find receiving difficult because we have to openly admit weakness. We often would rather do anything than ex-

No matter what I encounter today I will believe God can handle it.

pose our imperfections and needs. Romans 5:17 states the importance of receiving: "For if by the one man's offense death reigned through the one, much more those who receive abundance of grace and of the gift of righteousness will reign in life through the One, Jesus Christ" (NKJV).

Often wounded persons learn to achieve as a way of gaining approval and love. This makes receiving anything a real challenge. We frequently find helping much easier than being helped. Our desire to achieve actually expresses our need to be in control. Remember that the cross of Christ achieved all for us. The only thing left for us to do is "receive" Him. Go to Him daily with every need and ask that you may receive what you need to face your challenges and difficulties.

5. *Do not stop hoping!* Write the following statement on a card and put it in your purse or pocket: *No matter what I encounter today I will believe that God can handle it.* Read the card at meal times. Read it on the hour. Read it whenever you need to. We must never give up. Let us encourage you by saying that life really does get better. Do not give up hope!

Week 5

When Anger Leaves Me Depressed

Case in Point

"Angry? Not me! At least not until lately. It started out as mild irritability. Things that normally didn't bother me became a real pain. Usually when my two-year-old spills something, I tell myself, 'Everybody makes mistakes,' but recently it's all I can do to keep from screaming at the top of my lungs. When my husband is the least bit moody, I have fire in my eyes and murder in my voice. What's wrong with me? I'm just not acting like myself.

"Isn't it true that Christians aren't supposed to be angry? If so, God must be pretty upset with me. As a matter of fact, I'm disappointed in myself. Why can't I get a handle on my emotions? No matter what I try, the anger just seems to grow and grow. Is there any hope for ever understanding and overcoming my anger?"

Do you identify with this woman's need to control her anger? Our study this week will help you understand the role of anger and how it can help or hurt you and others.

This week you will consider ...
- what the Bible says about anger in relation to Christian living;
- why God created the emotion of anger;
- how anger can hurt both you and others.

What you will study
Day 1: What the Bible Says About Anger
Day 2: Can Anger Be a Positive Thing?
Day 3: When Anger Hurts Others
Day 4: When Anger Hurts Me
Day 5: Bringing My Anger to God

Memory verse
"Be angry, and yet do not sin; do not let the sun go down on your anger" (Eph. 4:26).

DAY 1
What the Bible Says About Anger

Purpose: To explain some biblical principles concerning anger

Passage: Read Proverbs 25:21-26 in preparation for today's study.

Anger often plays a major role in discouragement and depression. Sometimes it is the driving force behind a period of emotional darkness. Because of anger's significant contribution, we will be examining it for two full weeks. This week we will examine how anger, if not handled properly, can leave a person discouraged and depressed. Next week we will focus our attention on the practical aspects of how individuals can actually learn to control their anger. Let's begin this week by looking at what the Bible says about anger in the life of a Christian.

Take a moment and summarize what you think the Bible says about anger. Don't worry, this isn't a test. Just put your thoughts into words so you can examine them clearly.

_____

_____

_____

_____

_____

"When Saul saw how successful he was, he was afraid of him. But all Israel and Judah loved David, because he led them in their campaigns" (1 Sam. 18:15-16, NIV).

Saul, the first king of Israel, demonstrated the destructiveness of an anger problem. First Samuel 18:6-16 reveals how Saul's jealousy kindled his anger. Imagine the circumstances of the chapter. Saul was a giant of a man, the undisputed king of the nation, in his prime. David was a shepherd boy, totally loyal to his king. David killed Goliath. The people sang a song praising David, the hero of the day. Saul would have been wise to rejoice with his nation and the young David. Instead, Saul's jealousy led him to destructive anger.

Uncontrolled anger usually causes us to do things we would not normally do. When anger took over, Saul's good judgment left the building. Saul threw a spear at David and initiated the obsession that haunted the final 14 years of his reign as king. Saul spent the remainder of his life pursuing David and seeking his life. Out-of-control anger cost King Saul his peace, his sanity, and ultimately his life as well as the lives of his sons.

1. Anger is a powerful emotion and we need to exercise self-control.

"A hot-tempered man stirs up dissension, but a patient man calms a quarrel" (Prov. 15:18, NIV). Perhaps the most dominant teaching in the Scriptures concerning anger is that we should carefully control it. Anger and a lack of self-control got the best of Moses and kept him from entering the promised land as Israel's leader. In his anger and frustration, Moses failed to honor God before the people (see Num. 20:10-12).

Most of us would much rather live and work with people who are "slow to anger!" Perhaps you know an individual who is marked by this wonderful quality. Take a moment to list the names of three people who, through the years, have made a significant impression on you because of their patience in anger-provoking situations.

_____

_____

_____

2. Anger should not be the most prominent characteristic of our personalities.

When other people think about us, do they recall anger as our most defining trait? In the New Testament we read that anger should be taken off as part of the clothing of the old nature (see Col. 3:8).

The apostle Paul provided an up-close view of anger's dark side. In Galatians 5:19-21 he listed some characteristics of the flesh. Look at some of the words he used to characterize a life controlled by our desires.

Anger should be taken off as part of the clothing of our old natures.

hatred	contention	jealousy	envy
selfish ambition	dissension	outbursts of wrath	

As we read these words it becomes clear that God does not intend for Christians to live their lives in an angry tempest. In these verses Paul contrasted the Spirit and the flesh. He warned against the power of the flesh and characterized our struggle with it as war—an intense battle.

We must be cautious about the free expression of anger, especially when it comes from selfish motives. But can anger have a positive side? Are there ever times when it can be useful, helpful, righteous, and even productive?

3. We should be angry in some circumstances.

The Bible clearly endorses the healthy expression of anger. Anger has a place in the life of a Christian. This idea will be expanded in future weeks, but consider the following two points. Christians ought to be angered both when God's righteousness is compromised and when innocent people suffer.

Christians ought to be angered both when God's righteousness is compromised and when innocent people suffer.

When God's Righteousness Is Compromised

Anger due to offenses against God's holiness is a fairly frequent theme throughout the Bible.

Describe the examples of anger in the following verses.

Why was Moses angry? (Ex. 32:19) _____

_____

_____

Why was Jesus angry? (John 2:13-17) _____

_____

When Innocent People Suffer

The Lord is not blind to human suffering. God's people should be moved by the hardships and difficulties of others.

Describe the examples of anger in the following verses.

What stimulated the anger of Nehemiah? (Neh. 5:4-8) _____

_____

What provoked Jesus to anger in Mark 3:1-6? _____

_____

_____

God created anger as the response to wrong.

God created anger as the response to wrong. We feel anger when we perceive justice has been perverted. Imagine what would happen if we were incapable of anger. Evil would run rampant and we would be incapable of caring or doing anything about it.

Lord,
Anger is an emotion I would like to ignore. But I am realizing that part of my struggle with discouragement and depression is admitting the part that anger plays in my life. I confess to You that I have a difficulty with anger and I am not always sure how to deal with it. Neither am I sure how to have righteous anger. I want to surrender this area of my life to You. Please help me with my anger. Apart from You I can do nothing! Amen.

DAY 2
Can Anger Be a Positive Thing?

Purpose: To determine the benefits of healthy anger

Passage: Read Ephesians 4:26-27 in preparation for today's study.

No way! John thundered inside, as he listened to the Sunday morning sermon. He was reacting to the pastor's comment that anger can be helpful to believers. *I don't believe for one moment that anger should have any place in the life of a Christian,* he thought. John decided that he would schedule a time to talk with his pastor about the message on the benefits of anger.

As the pastor and John talked, it became clear why John viewed anger as he did. During the conversation he disclosed that during his childhood years both his dad and granddad were extremely volatile. Usually they physically expressed their anger and left a hole in the wall, a broken chair, or worse as a result of the episode. Therefore, John found it very difficult, if not impossible, to believe anger could have any positive value.

Because of their past experiences, many Christians view anger as entirely opposite to positive Christian living. Today we will explore what the Bible says about the healthy expression of anger and highlight a few practical guidelines.

Today's Scripture passage records some important words from the apostle Paul. He said, "Be angry, and yet do not sin; do not let the sun go down on your anger, and do not give the devil an opportunity" (Eph. 4:26-27). This passage contains key information for dealing with anger. First, we need to control our anger. Second, we need to realize that Satan's desire is for our anger to be unleashed.

Rather than using anger to accomplish our own ends, we need to focus our anger on accomplishing God's objectives. "Well," you might be asking, "how in the world do I do this?"

Rather than using anger to accomplish our own ends, we need to focus our anger on accomplishing God's objectives.

The Bible contains many examples of positive anger. Moses experienced anger because the Israelites were grossly unfaithful to God. Nehemiah's anger helped him address grievous sin among the people. Jesus felt anger because religious people disregarded both God and a fellow human being. Jesus cleared the temple because merchants were disregarding God and taking advantage of worshippers. All these examples demonstrate how anger can serve God's purposes.

These examples and Paul's words concerning anger demonstrate clearly that anger has value. Paul said an anger exists that is not sin.

How do you react to these examples of positive anger? Check any that apply or write your own response.

❏ I already knew about appropriate anger.
❏ I'm not sure I believe anger can ever be OK.
❏ I'm puzzled; how do I tell the difference?
❏ Wow! I've always believed I was sinning whenever I was angry.

_____

_____

Understanding Anger

When a person expresses anger, we can be certain they are trying to tell us something. Often anger can be a coded message, and the message may be difficult to understand. The idea of coding means the intended message is hidden. Because we fear honestly telling someone what we feel, we may hide the message. Anger is one of the chief ways we encode those feelings. The following three messages provide examples of de-coding devices to assist in understanding your anger or the anger of another.

Anger can be the way someone communicates that you have hurt him or her.

Ouch, That Hurts!

Anger can be the way someone communicates that you have hurt him or her. We live in a culture that does not encourage us to admit we feel pain. Rather, we have learned to hide the hurt and project strength. We use anger to:

1. avoid exposing our fragile hurt to those who may hurt us more;
2. guard ourselves from more pain by covering the hurt with a threat message, "I can hurt you back."

Can you think of a time when you used anger to tell someone he or she hurt you? Summarize that experience below.

_____

_____

_____

In your opinion does anger accurately express hurt, or does it tend to be counterproductive? Choose the best answer.

❏ Anger drives people away at a time when I need comfort and encouragement.
❏ Anger may protect me from getting hurt, but it results in greater pain.
❏ Anger works. Those who have hurt me understand and respond by drawing nearer to me.

No! That Is Wrong!

Jesus used anger in this way with the money-changers in the temple. They were obviously wrong, and wrongdoing deserves an adamant "No!" response from believers. Any time we see people abused or used we should feel anger. Like God, we must hate evil in whatever form it reveals itself, but we need to exercise self-control and express our anger in productive ways.

Rank the examples in the following list from the most positive (1) to the most destructive (4) use of anger to confront a wrong.

____ Sally discovered that her husband was committing adultery. She followed him to a motel and waited until he went inside. Then she slashed his tires.
____ Ben became so enraged over the ongoing killing of unborn babies that he planted a bomb outside an abortion clinic.
____ Melissa's mother continually criticized the way Melissa dressed, kept house, and cooked. Melissa finally became angry enough to confront her mother and tell her how the criticism hurt.
____ Richard felt that none of the leaders in the church were working as hard as he was. He left and went to another church.

Clearly Ben's expression of anger was the most destructive to himself, society, and the reputation of Christ. Melissa best used anger to respond to wrong. It's a toss up between Richard and Sally. Sally did property damage, but Richard damaged relationships. Of the four, which do you suppose would be least recognized as expressions of anger?

You Have Crossed My Personal Boundary!

Anger can indicate that someone has violated a boundary in a relationship. All forms of abuse include one person's violating another person's boundaries. For instance, sexual abuse of a minor does not permit the victim to have privacy concerning his or her own body. If a woman is verbally, emotionally, or physically battered, the offender is intruding on her personal boundaries.

A more common boundary violation occurs when one person attempts to control another by some form of emotional coercion such as guilt, intimidation, fear, or shame. When a mom tries to make her children clean up their rooms by saying God will be mad if they don't, she is manipulating by coercion. The children may complete the task but at the price of guilt and shame. When parents withhold affection from children as a means of control, they are practicing emotional coercion.

If a person grew up with boundary violations, as an adult he or she will have to learn to establish biblical boundaries. Establishing such boundaries takes time and effort, but a gracious and loving Heavenly Father definitely offers hope!

Anger can be a part of a healthy Christian's lifestyle. No longer must we view all anger as evil or damaging. Let's ask God to teach us about the healthy expression of anger.

Establishing boundaries takes time and effort, but a gracious and loving Heavenly Father definitely offers hope!

> *Lord,*
> *We want to submit to You our understanding and expression of anger. We need You to teach us the difference between acceptable and unacceptable anger. Your Word reveals that You express anger. Teach us to express anger in a righteous manner as You do. Cleanse us from self-centered anger. Amen.*

DAY 3
When Anger Hurts Others

Purpose: To understand how outbursts of anger cause discouragement and impact those we love

Passage: Read Matthew 15:18 in preparation for today's study.

A work crew broke a natural gas line in our area. Three men perished in the mighty fire that ensued. Ten thousand homes lost gas service. The scorching flames extended 25 yards in all directions. When I think of that fire, it represents for me a mental picture of anger "turned outward." Such anger behaves like an all-consuming fire, destroying anything in its path. Whoever stands in the way when anger explodes is sure to be hurt because anger explosions don't care about their targets. Anyone in the exploding person's path may be badly burned. Children, parents, friends, even a spouse can face the heat when anger pours forth.

You have probably heard the description that "depression is anger turned inward." We will consider the inward problem in tomorrow's study, but unchecked hostile anger can also contribute to depression and discouragement. How does "anger turned outward" contribute to discouragement?

Unchecked hostile anger can contribute to depression and discouragement.

- God did not design our bodies to have daily volcanic emotional eruptions. The body cannot continue to function in a healthy manner with frequent explosions of anger.
- Explosive anger interferes with the support we require from others. Our anger burns those closest to us. We drive away the people we need, and we pay the price in loneliness and more anger.

• Angry outbursts contribute to irresponsible living. The anger demonstrates our unwillingness to take responsibility for our personal problems. Blaming someone for our problems never leads to a healthy resolution.

The old adage, "Sticks and stones may break my bones but words will never hurt me," has never been true.

Can you list other ways that "anger turned outward" contributes to discouragement and depression?

_____

_____

_____

The purpose of today's study is to understand the effect of "anger turned outward" on us and those we love.

Anger Turned Outward Hurts Those Nearest Us

When the first nuclear explosion occurred, we had no idea of the fallout that would result. It was beyond our comprehension to understand that the explosion itself would release a form of radiation that destroys those separated from the initial explosion by many miles and years. Like a nuclear bomb, anger also has undetected fallout.

The most lethal result of explosive anger may be the "words" themselves. The old adage, "Sticks and stones may break my bones but words will never hurt me," has never been true. Words do hurt! As we spout forth anger, it spews deadly poison in the form of words. Name calling scars deeply. Words like "idiot," "stupid," and "clumsy" wound deeply, leaving lifetime scars. Tragically, we all have been both recipient and giver of harmful words.

Identify a time when you were the recipient of harmful words.

_____

Write a paragraph describing how you felt after hearing those words.

_____

_____

_____

_____

When our angry words hurt others, the best cure is to quickly admit our wrongdoing and ask forgiveness.

When our angry words hurt others, the best cure is to quickly admit our wrongdoing and ask forgiveness. Honesty does not eliminate the pain, but it does speed the healing. For instance, you may say to your child: "Honey, I am so sorry for yelling at you. That is not the way a daddy is supposed to act. When you are able, please forgive me. I am very sorry." Here's a simple phrase to remember when your anger explodes and injures: "When You Mess Up, Confess Up!"

Anger Turned Outward Pushes Others Away

Earlier we discovered how our words hurt those close to us. Unfortunately, it does not end there. Angry explosions also damage intimacy, causing distance between us and those we love. The hidden message in an angry outburst is "I dislike you." This may not have been the intended message, but it is the message people receive. When the message is given repeatedly with no attempts at reconciliation, relationships are badly damaged.

Angry explosions damage intimacy, causing distance between us and those we love.

Anger Turned Outward Does Not Solve Our Internal Problems

Jesus said, "But the things that proceed out of the mouth come from the heart, and those defile the man" (Matt. 15:18). Explosive anger does not address the internal problems of the heart (our innermost person). At best, an explosive episode allows a temporary tension release, but this release does not address the internal source of the problem.

Turning anger outward resembles an attempt to extinguish a campfire by fanning the flames. It gives you something to do but it does not put out the fire. When anger consistently pours forth in your life, learn to ask, "Where is this coming from?" That simple question allows you to take full responsibility for your anger while beginning to seek help for the answer.

Anger Turned Outward Demonstrates That I Have Been Hurt

One internal source of anger is relational pain. Someone hurt you. We all possess a reflexive tendency to strike back when someone hurts us. When you ask a three year old why she hit her sister she may answer, "She hurt me!" Even as adults when we get hurt, we hurt in return. Often that return hurt takes the form of "hostile anger." Our hurt has been boiling deep inside like hot lava inside the earth. At any given moment it erupts and spews molten lava on any and all standing near. It is our way of crying out, "I hurt!"

We all possess a reflexive tendency to strike back when someone hurts us.

> **Circle the thought you most identify with in today's study. On the lines provided tell why the thought has personal meaning for you.**
> • Anger turned outward hurts those nearest us.
> • Anger turned outward pushes others away.
> • Anger turned outward does not solve our internal problems.
> • Anger turned outward is evidence that I have been hurt.

_____

_____

_____

_____

Don't lose hope! Next week we'll take a "how-to" approach toward learning to control anger. The Bible has clear principles for growth!

DAY 4
When Anger Hurts Me

Purpose: To understand how anger toward yourself causes discouragement and depression

Passage: Read Romans 8:31-39 in preparation for today's study.

"For I am convinced that neither death, nor life, nor angels, nor principalities, nor things present, nor things to come, nor powers, nor height, nor depth, nor any other created thing, shall be able to separate us from the love of God, which is in Christ Jesus our Lord" (Rom. 8:38-39).

"Save me, O God! For the waters have come up to my neck. I sink in deep mire, where there is no standing; I have come into deep waters, where the floods overflow me. I am weary with my crying; My throat is dry; My eyes fail while I wait for my God" (Ps. 69:1-3, NKJV).

These stirring words well up from deep inside the psalmist—the cry of one feeling despair and hopelessness. Discouragement and depression often lead to such despair. One element of the torment is a deep sense of feeling unlovable, expressed as anger towards self. Someone who experiences this type of anger often finds it difficult to understand why. He or she may have lived this way for so long that it feels normal to be disappointed or angry with him or herself. Contrast the emotions expressed in the psalm with the promise expressed in today's Scripture reading.

Respond to the following from your reading of Romans 8:31-39:

1. Who is for us? (v. 31) _____

2. How has He shown us? (v. 32) _____

3. Who justifies us? (v. 33) _____

4. Who intercedes for us? (v. 34) _____

5. Can any person, thing, or situation separate us from the love of God? (vv. 35-39) ❏ yes ❏ no Explain your answer in your own words.

_____

_____

_____

_____

Romans 8:31-39 teaches us that the love of God in Christ Jesus our Lord is stronger than any person or situation we might encounter. Yet, in spite of the certainty of God's love, Christians often become their own worst enemies. This is particularly true if we have fallen into a pattern of self-condemnation. A constant stream of self-accusation can lead to discouragement and depression.

This type of anger is often difficult to detect for the one who faces it. If this type of self-condemnation describes you, you may have lived with it so long that it just feels normal to be disappointed or angry with yourself. Today we will identify some possible causes of "anger turned inward."

Your Family

Growing up in a home with either open or subtle rejection can result in self-disappointment or self-anger. When a child lives in a world of criticism, he or she learns to criticize both self and others. God intends for parents to prepare children for a deep, rich intimacy with Jesus. Sadly, that preparation does not always occur. Many children live in homes which lay no foundation for a personal relationship with a loving Lord. Without that foundation, children are more likely to develop a pattern of anger "turned inward."

A child may think: *If my parents don't love me, how can God love me?* Living in such a home can create the beginning of self-hate. The word *hate* is a strong word, yet, it accurately and best describes a depressed person's view of self. They no longer need parents to experience rejection; they reject themselves. They are convinced they are of no value to anyone—not to God, others, or themselves! Such a pattern of thinking frequently results in discouragement and depression.

God intends for parents to prepare children for a deep, rich intimacy with Jesus.

To what degree do you think you have or have not developed a pattern of self-criticism as described in the paragraphs above?

Very Self-Critical   Very Self-Accepting

Your School

For some, school strikes the first blow to a fragile and budding self-concept. The label "slow," "daydreamer," or "stupid" used repeatedly hammers away at a child's view of him or herself. This can also occur if the child is physically clumsy or encumbered by a learning disability. He or she may eventually dread and hate school because of the feelings it provokes. For the child to sit in class daily with those feelings is like the searing pain of a hot branding iron on his or her tender heart. The wound is deep and painful. All of this contributes to despair and depression.

Your Church

Wouldn't it be encouraging to know that if home and school are not safe and positive experiences that the church always will be? Unfortunately, yet often, this is not the case. A church can compound a child's rejection experience by supplying large doses of legalism. Legalism rests on a false promise that if you follow the rules perfectly you will earn favor with God. Legalism suffocates the love and grace bestowed by our merciful Heavenly Father. It misrepresents Him to the "little ones" entrusted to our care.

In a contrasting light, for children who experience pain both at home and school, church can be the place they first learn of God's love and acceptance—a safe haven from the storms overshadowing their young lives. It can also provide children with a sense of being loved that places them on the road to recovery and spiritual maturity. Let's pray that our churches will accept this challenge!

For children who experience pain both at home and school, church should be the place they first learn of God's love and acceptance.

Lord,
Make my church a safe and secure harbor for wounded children, a place where they can see how much You love them. I want my arms to become Your arms.

I want my words to become Your words. I want my life to be Your life to those children. Heal me Lord, so I may in turn be a source of Your healing to such hurting ones. May it be so Lord Jesus. Amen.

How Do You Talk to Yourself?

When you make a mistake, what do you say to yourself?

It may seem odd to include yourself as a contributor to anger turned inward, but many of us have learned to at least dislike if not hate ourselves. We picked up the messages from home, school, or church. Now we have taken over the job of chief-persecutor. We may be miles and years away from the original source of self-re-crimination and abuse, but we continue the process by self-criticism and perfectionism. We need to stop this form of self-abuse that keeps us chained to the past.

The way you talk to yourself strongly indicates if "you" continue the self-hate from the past. When you make a mistake, what do you say to yourself? (not what you may literally say, but rather what thoughts pop instantly into your mind about yourself).

Examples of how people can speak negatively to themselves appear below.

- I am such a loser!
- My parents were right, I'll never make it!
- Now I know why God could never love me!
- Just accept it, I'll never amount to anything!
- Why don't I just give up!

Can you identify with any of the statements above? ❏ yes ❏ no If so, write the statement you most identify with. If the ones above do not apply to you, then write what you do say to yourself when you fail to meet your own expectations.

_____

_____

_____

We have explored several "anger-turned inward" sources and briefly discussed the impact of each. The four we have mentioned appear below. Indicate the impact of each by circling the number that corresponds with the amount of influence it exerted on you. If you think of one we have not covered, write it also.

Very Little Impact   **Very Much Impact**

Family	1	2	3	4	5

School	1	2	3	4	5

Church	1	2	3	4	5	

You	1	2	3	4	5	

_____	1	2	3	4	5	

"There is therefore now no condemnation for those who are in Christ Jesus" (Rom. 8:1).

Father,
Thank You that You loved me and sent Your Son to die for me on the cross. Thank You that You will not condemn me, since I am in Your Son, Christ Jesus. I pray that You will help me day by day to think and talk about myself as You think and talk about me. Help me to make my church a place where others can find the grace, mercy, love, and acceptance offered in Jesus Christ. Amen.

DAY 5
Bringing My Anger to God

Purpose: To determine how anger impacts several areas of your life

Passage: Read Psalm 139:23-24 in preparation for today's study.

We have covered a lot of territory this week. The topic of anger may have reopened issues you need to address. Perhaps anger is a source of discouragement in your life. Let's begin today by asking God to guide us as we examine ways anger has impacted our lives. David expressed such a prayer with these words:

Search me, O God, and know my heart;
Try me and know my anxious thoughts;
And see if there be any hurtful way in me,
And lead me in the everlasting way (Ps. 139:23-24).

Pray the words of this psalm now. Ask the Lord to search you. Then ask for Him to lead you in His everlasting way. To be led in His everlasting way means God will show you how to live in line with His eternal truth.

You can always feel safe to allow the Lord to examine you, though you may have experienced rejection in the past when you allowed other people to get close. Often people who have negative experiences conclude, "I will never let anyone close to me again!" Our Heavenly Father never misuses our vulnerability. We can open ourselves up to Him without fear of rejection.

John, chapter 8 contains a touching example of our safety with God. In this passage, we encounter a woman not only caught in her sin but also put on public display (v. 3). The exposure of her sin was so shameful that it suffocated any self-re-

Our Heavenly Father never misuses our vulnerability. We can open ourselves up to Him without fear of rejection.

spect she might have had. What a terrible experience! The fact that the ones who exposed her had no intention of redeeming her (vv. 4-5) added to the shame. Yet Jesus dismissed the ones who highlighted her shame by pointing them to their own sinfulness (vv. 7-9).

Read the last part of verse 9 again. There she is, alone with Jesus and terribly ashamed. What would it be like to experience your sin totally brought to the light? When the Light is Jesus, the process is completely safe! Verses 10-11 record the words of reconciliation Jesus spoke to this shamed individual: " 'Woman, where are they? Did no one condemn you?' She said, 'No one, Lord.' And Jesus said, 'Neither do I condemn you; go your way. From now on sin no more.' "

The grace of God freed her from the shackles of shame and self-hate. He set her free—literally!

As you come to this time of asking God to search you, keep in mind the perfect safety of having our lives exposed before Him and brought to His light.

Day 2 addressed the fact that anger often serves to communicate different messages. How often do you use the following?

never   **frequently**

Ouch that hurts! (You are saying that someone has hurt you.)

         1   2   3   4   5

No! That is wrong! (You are reacting to something that God calls evil.)

         1   2   3   4   5

You have crossed my personal boundary! (You are abusing or coercing me.)

         1   2   3   4   5

Day 3 pointed out how outbursts of anger cause discouragement and hurt to those we love. How often do the following reactions reflect your anger?

never   **frequently**

I hurt those nearest to me.

         1   2   3   4   5

I push others away.

         1   2   3   4   5

I use my anger to temporarily release tension.

	1	2	3	4	5

I express my anger to demonstrate I have been hurt.

	1	2	3	4	5

Day 4 demonstrated how you may have fallen into a pattern of self-condemnation and become your own worst enemy! To what degree have you been negatively impacted by each of the following sources? Did you come to conclude that you were of little value based on these sources? How frequently do you experience anger turned inward as a result of these sources?

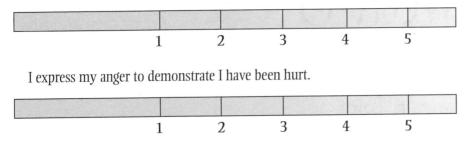

never   frequently

Family   1   2   3   4   5

School   1   2   3   4   5

Church   1   2   3   4   5

_____   1   2   3   4   5
(Other)

As you prayed and reviewed what you studied this week, what did you discover? What areas of your life are most obviously impacted by anger? List those areas below.

_____

_____

Next week we will suggest some specific strategies for learning to control your anger. The assessment above provides a solid foundation for next week's action steps.

Dear Father,
Thank You for faithfully searching me, knowing me, and leading me. I know that You always have my best interest in mind. Reveal Your heart to me as I work through times of discouragement and depression. I place all of my hope in You. Prepare me as I seek to work with my own anger next week. Remind me that "You are with me" during this unique time in my life. Amen.

WEEK 6
Controlling Your Anger

Case in Point

Shelley was depressed over her lack of close friends. She talked with a lay counselor at her church about her relationship problems. As Shelley's friendships developed, the friends became more and more distant. The pattern made no sense to Shelley, but as she worked with the counselor to uncover the reason, Shelley realized she had a definite problem with anger.

The counselor helped Shelley to see that whenever she began to get close to a new friend, she took that person for granted and became angry over insignificant things. For Shelley, this was simply her way of communicating. After all, she grew up in a critical family. She believed her critical words were just "telling it like it is."

After discussing several key biblical principles with her counselor, Shelley understood that she needed to control her aggressiveness with others. She is still quick to give her opinion in her communication style but is becoming a kinder and gentler friend.

This week we will introduce ways to manage anger so that we can develop the intimacy with others that God intends.

This week you will ...
- explore ways to control anger;
- identify two types of anger, requiring two different types of control;
- discover hope by growing in perseverance and prayer.

What you'll study
Day 1: Two Types of Anger
Day 2: Aggressive Anger: Learning to Control It
Day 3: Passive Anger: Learning to Speak Up
Day 4: Perseverance and Prayer
Day 5: Hatred, Resentment, and Vengeance

Memory verse
"He who is slow to anger has great understanding,
But he who is quick-tempered exalts folly" (Prov. 14:29).

DAY 1
Two Types of Anger

Purpose: To identify the two types of anger

Passage: Read Colossians 3:8 in preparation for today's study.

Last week we observed how improperly managed anger can leave a person discouraged and depressed. This week we want to explore a "how-to" approach to controlling anger.

Hope definitely exists for you to control anger.

If you (or someone you know) have found yourself frustrated at the prospect of overcoming angry feelings and the sadness they produce, we want to offer you a way out of the predicament. Hope definitely exists for you to control anger.

First, let's take a look at the two main types of anger, representing two very different groups of angry people locked in a discouraging place. We must be careful to separate these groups in our thinking, since each requires a different remedy.

The Aggressive Person

Aggressive people attempt to work with others using this slogan: "Do it my way!" They frequently get what they want, but all too often leave a trail of hurting people in their wake. They believe that harsh words and intimidation are acceptable methods to accomplish their objectives.

Aggressiveness can be a positive quality when a person is led and controlled by the Spirit of God. We could argue that many of the great saints in Scripture were quite aggressive. Paul offers a prominent New Testament example of healthy aggressiveness, but take a look at him before the Lord took control of his life. In the Book of Acts prior to his conversion, Paul aggressively attempted to halt the growth of the early church:

1. Underline words indicating Paul's aggression.

[Paul], still breathing threats and murder against the disciples of the Lord, went to the high priest (Acts 9:1).

For you have heard of my former manner of life in Judaism, how I used to persecute the church of God beyond measure, and tried to destroy it; and I was advancing in Judaism beyond many of my contemporaries among my countrymen, being more extremely zealous for my ancestral traditions (Gal.1:13,14).

Aggressiveness can be a positive quality when a person is led and controlled by the Spirit of God.

2. What do you think Paul was trying to gain by acting aggressively?

_____

_____

_____

3. If you use aggression, take a moment to list what you gain from it. If you do not use aggression, describe what someone you know gains from acting aggressively.

_____

_____

God changed Paul—and He can change you too!

If you are an aggressive person, you can learn to channel your aggression in positive ways. Note that in the previous passage (Gal. 1:13), Paul described his "former manner of life." God changed him—and He can change you too!

Do you remember Shelley at the beginning of this unit? She was a young woman who had difficulty understanding why her friends backed away from her. She had a strong aggressive streak. Although she frequently got her way, she left a trail of would-be friends in her wake. Tomorrow we will study the steps suggested by the counselor to help Shelly control her aggressiveness while learning to be a gentler friend. Shelly took to heart Paul's instruction in Colossians 3:8:

> But now you also, put them all aside: anger, wrath, malice, slander, and abusive speech from your mouth.

The Passive Person

Like the aggressive person, the passive person operates using an equally harmful slogan: "I guess I got it wrong!" Passive people, like aggressive ones, throw a lot of punches, but with one major difference, they usually hit themselves!

Passive people tend to be their own worst enemies. They allow situations to develop in which they know they are being stepped on, but they fail to stand up for themselves in an appropriate manner. In time, when pushed too far, they may respond with passive aggression.

Passive aggression is a stealth form of retaliation and can occur with very few people knowing about it. Kate enjoyed cooking when she was first married. But her husband Andy constantly criticized her for minor mistakes. Nothing was ever quite good enough. At first Kate blamed herself. *I have to try harder*, she thought. Then as time passed, she became angry. Most people have limits, and Kate was no exception. She began to retaliate in subtle ways: she avoided cooking his favorite meals; she frequently prepared supper "slightly well done," and so on!

Andy and Kate could have avoided this scenario in several ways. Of course, Andy could have been more encouraging and less hurtful with his comments. From the onset Kate could have responded directly to her husband's criticism by lovingly and firmly confronting Andy's unkind words.

Can a passive person learn to speak up? Yes!

Can a passive person learn to speak up? Yes! On day 3 we'll observe how Kate learned to speak clearly and openly to Andy.

Father,
Help me to deal with my anger. Where I tend to be aggressive, teach me to temper it with love. Where I tend to be passive, teach me to practice assertiveness and to stand up for both You and myself. I know that You created anger. I cannot escape it, Lord, so teach me to manage it for Your glory. Amen.

DAY 2
Aggressive Anger: Learning to Control It

Purpose: To discover ways to control aggressive anger in order to develop the intimacy with others God intended

Passage: Read 2 Timothy 2:22 in preparation for today's study.

Paul's second letter to Timothy contains three important principles that can revolutionize the life of any anger-prone person. When understood properly, angry individuals can channel their aggressiveness in healthy ways and enjoy the intimacy with others God intended.

Have you ever thought to yourself: *Why can't I overcome my anger and aggressiveness? I'm ruining my relationships by these hurtful actions.* Remember Shelley from day 1? Using 2 Timothy 2:22 as a base, her counselor pointed out three key ideas for dealing with anger. The apostle Paul puts them forth in clear succession. Let's look at each phrase of the verse and paraphrase it.

We can channel our aggressiveness in healthy ways and enjoy the intimacy with others God intended.

1. The first phrase is, "Flee from youthful lusts."

To flee seems a wise choice when we encounter someone who is bigger, meaner, and angrier than we are. *Flee* means *to run away from something to be feared.* Lusts are controlling urges. Whether the urge is for food, sexual gratification, or to indulge our anger, the same fact holds true; if we remain in the presence of a lust—a controlling urge—we will lose the war. Safety comes in getting away from the urge. But where are we to go? Jesus' words speak powerfully to the issue.

> "When an evil spirit comes out of a man, it goes through arid places seeking rest and does not find it. Then it says, 'I will return to the house I left.' When it arrives, it finds the house unoccupied, swept clean and put in order. Then it goes and takes with it seven other spirits more wicked than itself, and they go in and live there. And the final condition of that man is worse than the first. That is how it will be with this wicked generation" (Matt. 12:43-45, NIV).

The principle Jesus taught is not complicated. Nature abhors a vacuum in both the physical and spiritual realms. We must fill our lives with biblical and positive thoughts and behaviors or Satan will attempt to fill them with something less than wholesome. We need to identify positive and God-honoring character traits. Then, with prayerful consistency, we need to practice them until they become patterns in our lives.

You can establish certain personal limits to prevent damaging relationships with your aggressive anger. These habits are developed over time. It takes approximately 90 days for most people to develop a new pattern in their lives. Note the wisdom of the following proverb.

It takes approximately 90 days for most people to develop a new pattern in their lives.

A hot-tempered man stirs up strife,
But the slow to anger pacifies contention (Prov. 15:18).

Complete the statements below to identify positive characteristics you need to develop.

When I start to get angry I will _____.

When I start to get angry I will _____.

When I start to get angry I will _____.

When I start to get angry I will separate myself from the situation for a short time, pray, and collect my thoughts.

Perhaps you identified practical actions such as, "When I start to get angry I will count to 10," or "When I start to get angry I will separate myself from the situation for a short time, pray, and collect my thoughts." (Note: If you are married, it is best to leave the room rather than the house!)

2. Paul's second phrase is: "Pursue righteousness, faith, love and peace."

We could paraphrase the apostle's words this way: "seek to grow spiritually." Different people have many different definitions of spiritual growth. Consider this simple approach. Growth happens whenever you "flee" or turn away from one way of living and replace it with another characteristic behavior.

To grow spiritually, we always need to have a goal. Remember Paul said in Colossians 3:8, "Put them all aside: anger, wrath, malice, slander, and abusive speech from your mouth." He followed that instruction with a reminder that after we have taken off our "coat" of anger, we should put on other behaviors:

> As those who have been chosen of God, holy and beloved, put on a heart of compassion, kindness, humility, gentleness and patience (Col. 3:12).

In the categories below, list some personal growth goals to help you to control your anger.

A. Righteousness—For example: I will begin each day by thanking God for making me a new creation in Christ (2 Cor. 5:17).

Your righteousness goals:

_____

_____

_____

I will begin each day by thanking God for making me a new creation in Christ.

B. Faith—For example: I will pray daily for God to give me success, and I will resist "forcing" my way.

Your faith goals:

_____

_____

C. Love—For example: I will memorize Matthew 22:37-39: " 'You shall love the Lord your God with all your heart, and with all your soul, and with all your mind.' This is the great and foremost commandment. The second is like it, 'You shall love your neighbor as yourself.' "

Your love goals:

Consider saying, "I was wrong; I'm sorry; please forgive me."

_____

_____

_____

D. Peace—For example: consider if there are any relationships you need to be mend. Follow the simple yet profound phrase, "I was wrong; I'm sorry; please forgive me."

Your peace goals:

_____

_____

_____

3. The third phrase is: "With those who call on the Lord from a pure heart."

We could paraphrase Paul's words to mean, "be accountable to healthy Christians." The Lord's plan is for us to live in relationship with, confide in, and be accountable to other believers. You can be certain that just as you have needs in your life, your friends have burdens in their lives too. It is a steady process of growth as day by day we become more like Jesus.

If you struggle with anger, list the names of several Christians with whom you can share and pray. If acted-out anger is not a problem for you, list the names of three people for whom you can pray.

1. _____

2. _____

3. _____

Lord,
Sometimes I do not even understand myself. I act aggressively and I hurt the very people I care most about in life. Help me to implement the teachings of your Word. Guide me as I seek to establish godly boundaries, grow spiritually, and be accountable to healthy Christians. I know that I must depend upon You for growth. Help me to trust You with my anger. In Jesus' name. Amen.

The Lord's plan is for us to live in relationship with, confide in, and be accountable to other believers.

DAY 3
Passive Anger: Learning to Speak Up

Purpose: To discover ways to control passive anger to develop close and honest relationships and to experience the peace that God provides

Passage: Read Proverbs 15:1; 18:13 in preparation for today's study.

Today we will concentrate on the passive person, one who experiences a considerable amount of inner conflict while struggling to experience the calm and quietness of God. While aggressive persons wage war outwardly and create tension for others around them, passive persons suffer inner conflict and anxiety. Although persons with passive personalities generally do not act in an outwardly aggressive manner, as time passes they may eventually respond with passive aggression. If eventually a passive person is backed into a corner—watch out!

Remember Kate in day 1 of this week? She continually found herself in situations where she felt stepped on, but she did not stand up for herself in a biblically appropriate manner. She allowed anger and resentment to build up and became passive aggressive toward her husband, expressing her anger in quiet, subtle, and dishonest ways.

Finally, Kate talked to a trustworthy friend in her church, explaining that she honestly loved her husband and desired to be a godly wife, but her anger at his criticism and unkind words had become too much to bear. Kate's friend, Sharon, showed Kate some biblically-based truths and principles about anger. Sharon also prayed with Kate over the next few weeks as she learned how to lovingly confront her husband.

> **Practice your skills as a counselor. What principles would you share with Kate in this situation?**

_____

_____

_____

Andy was surprised at first! From his perspective, he had been trying to help Kate improve herself. Later, however, Andy recognized how the criticism had hurt her. He was genuinely grieved over his lack of sensitivity to the one he loved. Andy acknowledged that he was wrong, apologized to Kate, and asked for her to forgive him.

Not every person will respond positively, as Andy did. If you find yourself in a similar predicament in your relationships, employ these key principles as you confront. They enhance the concept of clear and open communication.

Good communication includes three elements: understanding, listening, and talking.

Good Communication

Good communication includes three elements: understanding, listening, and talking. Communication breaks down when any one of these elements is missing.

Understanding—Determine how the other person views the subject under discussion. If you comprehend that position from the beginning, communication will be off to a great start.

Listening—Rare indeed is the person who doesn't appreciate a good listener. Before you begin talking, make sure you hear what the other person has to say. Proverbs 18:13 says, "He who gives an answer before he hears, it is folly and shame to him." Listen! Then you'll know what to say!

Make sure you hear what the other person has to say.

Talking—When conversing with another, speak clearly, honestly, and directly. State your position in a respectful and non-emotional manner. This idea is affirmed in Proverbs 15:1, "A gentle answer turns away wrath, but a harsh word stirs up anger." Make your point truthfully, and stay on the subject with the other person during the course of the conversation.

A Simple Plan for Speaking Clearly and Openly

The following simple plan can help when you need to speak clearly and openly. Use these three questions to plan a conversation with someone whose words and actions have left you feeling hurt or angry.

1. What did the person do or say that made you angry?

Try to be as specific as possible and limit yourself to one subject at a time. Avoid the use of terms like "you always," or "you never." It is best not to attack the person but rather to point out how his or her actions have made you feel.

- "When you schedule so many jobs on one day, I feel overwhelmed."
- "When you criticize my cooking, I feel like I'm failing as a wife."
- "When you complain about how old the furniture is, I feel like I'm not providing adequately as a husband."

2. What sort of changes are you hoping to see?

Be prepared to offer suggestions in regard to the changes you would like to occur. This approach reduces strong emotional exchanges and helps the other person to consider the fact that there may be a simple solution to the problem. Anticipation of change suggests hope for the relationship rather than discouragement. For example, when Kate explained to Andy that she needed him to affirm her, he understood that Kate still loved him. In fact, he now realizes how much she values his opinion and that his words have tremendous impact.

3. What might be the result if the situation does not change?

Our words and actions always have consequences. When speaking to someone clearly and openly about an important matter, identify the potential problems that will result if the situation remains the same. Here are two examples.

Our words and actions always have consequences.

An employee explains to his supervisor that the amount of work scheduled each day is leaving him overwhelmed. If the workflow remains unchanged, the consequence may be that he looks for another job.

Arlene explained to her mother that if she refuses to use the car seat, Arlene will no longer allow her to drive with her grandson.

Develop an Action Plan:

An action must be clear and focused. Use the following form to develop an action plan.

I need to speak with _____ about the following problem.

1. What did the person do or say that made you angry or hurt?

_____

_____

2. What sort of changes are you hoping to see?

_____

_____

3. What might be the result if the situation does not change?[1]

_____

_____

DAY 4
Perseverance and Prayer

Purpose: To discover how to experience God's joy even during those times you are troubled

Passage: Read Psalm 4 in preparation for today's study.

David maintained hope and joy in the Lord even when confronted by people and situations he could not change.

Yesterday we learned principles for confronting others when we are either hurt or angry. Perhaps you are saying: "Wait just a minute! What if I can't speak up? What if I talk to my boss and he says, 'If you think you have too much work to do here, you can find another job!' "?

Today let's examine those times when healthy assertiveness simply is not possible. Some wives attempt to confront their husbands as Kate did but do not receive the same positive response Andy gave. They may have tried repeatedly without seeing any change. Such "out-of-our-control" situations occur in many different type relationships—children who do not listen to their parents; parents who do not listen to their adult children; brothers and sisters who refuse to communicate. Examples also occur in the workplace: managers who do not listen to employees; coworkers who do not listen to one another. Let's take a look at David's response when he was confronted by men he could not change to determine ways a person can maintain hope and joy in the Lord.

When You Can't Speak to a Person, Speak to God

This principle appears in Psalm 4:4-5: when you can't speak to a person, speak clearly and openly to God! When we encounter problems with difficult people, it helps to remember that David dealt with an entire kingdom of personalities! To be sure, some were men and women of God, but others were not. In fact, David described these men as attacking his honor, loving what is worthless, and seeking to deceive (see Ps. 4:2).

David knew he could make his complaints known to God and be heard.

David could not reason with these individuals. Although he was king, he did not have the option of speaking clearly, honestly, and directly with them and waiting for a fair and positive response. David was a righteous man, so undoubtedly he had tried this approach in the past. But in all his efforts he had only learned the true intents of their hearts.

So what do godly men or women do in a situation like this? They follow David's example; they talk to God and they pray. David stated confidently in verse 3, "the Lord has set apart the godly man for Himself; The Lord hears when I call to Him." David knew he could make his complaints known to God and be heard. In Psalm 4 the Lord taught David how to respond when he could not reason with people.

The instruction David received from God contains three key points. They appear in verses 4 and 5 and apply equally well to our present-day situations.

1. Tremble, and do not sin.

Do you ever wonder why the many translations of God's Word read differently? Often the English language poorly expresses the meaning of the original words. The *New King James Version* translates the first word in Psalm 4:4 as "Be angry." The *King James Version* says, "Stand in awe." The *New International Version* reads, "In your anger." Why these differences in translation? The highly expressive Hebrew word means, "Tremble with anger." It pictures a person frozen in place, trembling with emotion. Paul quoted this verse in Ephesians 4:26: "Be angry, and yet do not sin." It is a fact that people may cause us anger by their words and actions. Although our anger may be justified, we must practice self-restraint. When aroused with anger, God wants us to exercise self-control. The well-known phrase, "two wrongs do not make a right," expresses this same teaching.

Describe a time when you were angry and wanted to retaliate. What did you do about your anger?

_____

_____

"Two wrongs do not make a right."

_____

_____

2. Meditate in your heart upon your bed, and be still.

God wants us to think through the situation with Him. Confess to Him the extent of your anger. Honestly express your outrage to God with full confidence that He hears. After all, doesn't God love what is good and right? Often it is wise to wait at least a day before responding to a person or situation that has provoked anger. The sense of this verse is, "Carefully think through the situation with God and wait patiently before responding."

Realistically we can learn to exercise patience because we know God. Peter expressed the principle in 1 Peter 5:7, "Casting all your anxiety upon Him, because He cares for you."

When I offer my next sacrifice to God, I want to do so with hands that have not sinfully retaliated.

List several things that trouble you today.

1. _____

2. _____

3. _____

Are you willing to cast these burdens on Him?

❑ Yes ❑ No If not, why?_____

_____

3. Offer the sacrifices of righteousness, and trust in the Lord.

The Lord wants us to live life with a clean conscience. Trust Him to fight for you since no situation we face is too difficult for Him. Perhaps David thought to himself, *When I offer my next sacrifice to God, I intend to do so with hands that have not sinfully retaliated.*

Experiencing His Joy and Peace

We have seen how David felt anger at certain men and yet exercised self-control in His response. He thoughtfully processed the situation. He expressed his emotion—sometimes vehemently (see Ps. 22:1-2). Then he chose to trust in the Lord. As a result, David experienced a joy that exceeded any material gain those who opposed him obtained through their unrighteousness.

David experienced peace as a result of following the Lord's instruction.

Thou hast put gladness in my heart,
More than when their grain and new wine abound (Ps. 4:7).

The peace that David experienced as a result of following the Lord's instruction appears in the concluding verse of Psalm 4. Surrounded by individuals who were attacking his honor and deceitfully going after worthless things, David got a good night's sleep!

In peace I will both lie down and sleep,
For Thou alone, O Lord, dost make me to dwell in safety (Ps. 4:8).

Take a moment and ask the Lord to help you to make good responses to the problems you may be facing in relationships other people. If you are unable to speak with a person clearly and openly, talk to God about it! Thank Him for His love and protection.

DAY 5
Hatred, Resentment, and Vengeance

Purpose: To determine to get rid of hatred, resentment, and vengeance

Passage: Read Leviticus 19:17-18 in preparation for today's study.

During the last two weeks we have focused on a major cause of discouragement and depression—anger. In week 5 we discussed how harboring anger can result in depression, leaving both the angry individual and those around him or her discouraged and depressed. It followed sensibly that week 6 was devoted to the crucial topic, "Controlling Your Anger." We searched God's Word for answers and learned He does offer hope for the angry person!

Looking Back at Days 1-4

1. Two Types of Anger
Since two types of angry people exist, we require two different remedies for the problem. Aggressively angry people often get what they want, but leave behind an unfortunate trail of hurting people. Passively angry people, on the other hand, tend to be their own worst enemies, causing themselves considerable pain by failing to speak up about the situations or actions which anger them. In the end they also leave behind a trail of confused and hurting people.

2. Aggressive Anger: Learning to Control It
In 2 Timothy 2:22 we considered three principles for controlling aggressive anger: set clear boundaries; seek to grow spiritually; and establish accountability to healthy Christians.

3. Passive Anger: Learning to Speak Up
A passive person can experience God's peace by following a simple plan for speaking clearly and honestly. We identified three elements of good communication and developed an action plan for speaking to someone whose words and actions result in hurt or anger.

A person can receive God's joy and peace even when it is impossible to respond to the people causing the anger.

4. Perseverance and Prayer
Finally, we learned how a person can receive God's joy and peace even when it is impossible to respond to the people who are causing the anger. In Psalm 4, David conveyed to us what he learned from God about responding properly to his experience of anger. He refused to sin, talked to God about the situation, and placed his trust in the Lord.

A Final Word on Controlling Anger

We've examined three different ways to control anger which related to the aggressive person, the passive person, and the individual who can turn only to God.

In Leviticus 19:17-18, God instructed His people concerning hatred and anger. This passage is especially helpful today because it encourages us to keep our hearts free from resentment and grudges against others that can ultimately hinder our happiness and leave us discouraged as we seek to walk with God.

> You shall not hate your fellow countryman in your heart; you may surely reprove your neighbor, but shall not incur sin because of him. You shall not take vengeance, nor bear any grudge against the sons of your people, but you shall love your neighbor as yourself; I am the Lord (Lev. 19:17-18).

Hatred and bitterness in our heart toward others is sin.

Let's break down the verses into four important points as we seek to deal with anger. These points, three of which are commands, have the capacity to significantly change how we relate to other people.

1. "You shall not hate your fellow countryman in your heart."

God says we are not to live our lives with hatred in our hearts toward anybody. This is not a difficult task concerning most people, but what about the man who said _____, or the woman who did _____. With some individuals we find this command increasingly difficult to obey. Yet the Lord continues with an important idea, a statement that corresponds to information we learned in day 3 about speaking up. God says, "You may surely reprove your neighbor, but shall not incur sin because of him" (Lev 19:17). God knows that at times the words and actions of others will require us to reprove them and speak up when their sin affects us. However, God also says that hatred and bitterness in our heart toward others is sin and we are to avoid it.

> **Take a moment to list the names of anyone that might hold a place of hatred and resentment in your heart. If necessary use initials or your own code for the names.**
>
> 1. _____
>
> 2. _____
>
> 3. _____
>
> **If you cannot speak with one or more of these individuals, refer back to day 3 and develop an action plan.**

2. "You shall not take vengeance, nor bear any grudge against the sons of your people."

Clearly the Lord does not desire for retaliation to be a part of our daily lives. Consequently, it makes no sense to bear grudges since, in obedience to God, we will never take vengeance. People bear grudges in the hope of one day "getting even." Once the idea of future retaliation is removed, grudges can be left at the Lord's feet.

Cultivate the pattern of leaving difficulties with people in God's hands.

Paul said in Romans 12:19, "Never take your own revenge, beloved, but leave room for the wrath of God, for it is written, 'Vengeance is Mine, I will repay,' says the Lord." If necessary, cultivate a new pattern of leaving difficulties with people in God's hands.

"But if your enemy is hungry, feed him, and if he is thirsty, give him a drink; for in so doing you will heap burning coals upon his head." Do not be overcome by evil, but overcome evil with good (Rom. 12:20-21).

Is there anything good you can do for the people described in the above verse? Consider some of the following ideas:

- Invite them to lunch.
- Invite them over for dinner.
- Compliment them on an accomplishment.
- Write a letter of reconciliation.
- Offer to help them with a task or chore.
- Offer to help them with a financial burden.
- Let them know you pray for them.

3. "You shall love your neighbor as yourself."

Most of us are happiest when we know others like us. We certainly do not want others to feel hatred, desire retaliation, or bear grudges toward us. The Lord wants us to treat others as we want to be treated. Remember Jesus' "new commandment." Our obedience to His commandment is not based on others' words or actions, but on our desire to walk with the Lord and do His will.

"A new commandment I give to you, that you love one another, even as I have loved you, that you also love one another" (John 13:34).

4. "I am the Lord."

These four words are words of hope! You can be certain that any task God asks you to accomplish will be the right thing to do and will work out best for you. Believing this is the essence of trust. Use the following prayer to guide your response to God.

Believing that any task God asks you to accomplish will be the right thing to do and will work out best for you is the essence of trust.

Dear Lord,
Thank you for giving me Your Word. I find forgiving people who have wronged me to be very difficult. To be kind and seek their best seems even more difficult. Please help me to love and serve those who have hurt me. Thank You that You are the Lord and You always have my best interests in mind. Amen.

[1]Ideas for questions in this section came from unpublished class notes, George Fox University, Clark Campbell, Phd., n.d., n.p., n. pag.

Week 7

Stress and the Role of Health

Case in Point

Eight a.m. and Todd already feels tired. The list of tasks he needs to accomplish at work today seems endless. A mountain of paperwork waits on his desk. He can't even think about the rest of the week. As he drives the familiar road to work, the more he thinks about his job the more exhausted he becomes. Todd feels like a runner at the two-mile marker of a marathon with a long, hard 24 miles to go.

At home his list of chores also continues to grow. His inability to complete them causes friction with his wife. His lack of time with the kids leaves him guilt-ridden. Todd feels that he is failing in most of life's significant areas.

Lately he's also been plagued by physical problems. His body cries out to him through headaches, back and shoulder tightness, stomach problems, and exhaustion. So what is Todd to do? Friends encourage him to slow down, and he knows it's good advice, but how can he?

This week we will explore some ideas on managing stress. Stress often manifests itself in depression and discouragement. We will also address the role our bodies play in our spiritual lives.

This week you will ...
- explore what the Bible says about health-related problems;
- examine the role of failed expectations in managing stress;
- determine how a chemical imbalance can result in depression;
- discover how to approach life in a balanced manner.

What you'll study
Day 1: The Bible and Health Problems
Day 2: What Is a Chemical Imbalance?
Day 3: Stress and Overload
Day 4: Stress and Medical Problems
Day 5: Balanced Living

Memory verse
"Paul, an apostle of Christ Jesus according to the commandment of God our Savior, and of Christ Jesus, who is our hope" (1 Tim. 1:1).

DAY 1
The Bible and Health Problems

Purpose: To develop a biblical perspective on health-related problems

Passage: Read Job 1:20-22; 2:3-13 in preparation for today's study.

Health problems can lead to discouragement and depression. If you are facing a terminal illness or have a friend or loved one with this diagnosis, discouragement and depression are understandable reactions. Persons with debilitating illnesses or long-term conditions, such as paralysis or arthritis, have cause to feel these same emotions.

Although serious medical issues certainly are justifiable reasons to feel down emotionally, often we overlay health issues with spiritual guilt. Today we will focus on health problems from a biblical perspective. Look for insights as you continue your own discovery of hope or as you seek to support others struggling with discouragement and depression.

Consider the following three questions:

1. Are health problems God's judgment for sin?
2. Do unhealthy people simply need more faith?
3. What is God's attitude toward the sick?

1. Are Health Problems God's Judgment for Sin?

If you struggle with poor health or can reflect back on a time when you did, you probably wondered if your health problems were related to your spiritual life. After all, we often hear that bodily afflictions are God's judgment for sin. In addition, when we are struggling and need God the most, poor health may leave us feeling distant from the One to whom we have prayed for health.

Have you ever wondered if your health problems were related to your spiritual life?

Various trials confronted Job as he tried to live a righteous life. Health problems severely tested Job's faith. At the beginning of the story, the book described Job as a man of high integrity and character. "There was a man in the land of Uz, whose name was Job, and that man was blameless, upright, fearing God, and turning away from evil" (Job 1:1).

Suddenly he faced the greatest trials of his life. First, Job lost all his possessions: oxen, sheep, camels, servants—even his sons and daughters. Job was deeply grieved, but despite all that he lost, he did not sin nor blame God (see 1:22).

Second, Job lost his health. His entire body was covered with sore boils to such an extent that his friends could not recognize him. Just the sight of him brought them to tears (see 2:7-13).

If sin causes ill-health, Job would have been physically perfect! Instead of perfection, however, Job had to defend himself to his friends who claimed his sin caused the boils. At the conclusion of the book, Job's faith in God shined through. How did Job discover hope in his despair? Job discovered God in a new way!

"I have heard of Thee by the hearing of the ear;
But now my eye sees Thee" (Job 42:5).

Job's friends could have been helpful to him in his distress. Because of the naturally discouraging circumstances, Job needed comfort from his friends rather than rebuke. When God places us in the lives of people who are suffering ill-health, we have a responsibility to offer support and encouragement. While an undisciplined lifestyle can result in health problems, like Job, people frequently face sickness and disease over which they have absolutely no control.

God places us in the lives of people suffering ill-health to offer support and encouragement.

Can you recall a time in your life when you were extremely sick?
❑ Yes ❑ No

If so, describe the circumstances.

_____

_____

Was any one person especially helpful at that time? Explain.

_____

_____

What passages of Scripture did God use to restore your hope?

_____

_____

_____

2. Do Unhealthy People Simply Need More Faith?

Ultimately, all sickness can be traced to the garden of Eden. As a result of Adam and Eve's sin, death became our enemy. Now our bodies are susceptible to sickness and disease. With the exceptions of Enoch and Elijah, every man and woman in the past has died.

God certainly wants us to pray for those who are sick, but if faith cured all illnesses, many people would have lived forever! We would expect the great men and women of faith to have been unusually healthy! Even the New Testament provides accounts of some very strong Christians who went through life with various illnesses. Look at Paul and Timothy. Paul stated that God had given him a "thorn in the flesh" so that the great revelations he had received would not go to his head and make him proud (see 2 Cor. 12:7).

God does heal the sick and prayers of faith do count with Him.

Paul also offered Timothy advice in regard to health concerns. Paul told his son in the faith, "use a little wine for the sake of your stomach and your frequent ailments" (1 Tim. 5:23). If Paul were alive today, he surely would have recommended an over-the-counter medication with fewer side effects.

God does heal the sick and prayers of faith do count with Him. However, the converse is not true. Great prayers of faith do not always result in a cure. Until the Lord returns, death will ultimately overtake the greatest prayer warriors.

3. What Is God's Attitude Toward the Sick?

Jesus sometimes healed to demonstrate His power and authority to forgive sins (see Mark 2:10-11), but He also healed simply out of compassion. "When He went ashore, He saw a great multitude, and felt compassion for them, and healed their sick" (Matt 14:14).

Second Corinthians 1:3-4 indicates God's compassion toward those who are afflicted. "Blessed be the God and Father of our Lord Jesus Christ, the Father of mercies and God of all comfort; who comforts us in all our affliction so that we may be able to comfort those who are in any affliction with the comfort with which we ourselves are comforted by God" (2 Cor. 1:3-4).

We are called to minister God's comfort to those who are facing any affliction.

The passage contains three important lessons about God's comfort:

1. He is the God of all comfort.
2. He comforts us in all our affliction.
3. He has prepared us to be ministers of His comfort.

Notice that we are called to minister God's comfort to those who are facing any affliction. Even if we've never faced the same affliction a friend may be experiencing, we can still offer them support, encouragement, and comfort.

List areas in your life in which you are facing difficulty:

1. _____

2. _____

3. _____

Take a moment to thank the Lord that He looks on your afflictions with compassion.

List ways God has comforted you.

1. _____

2. _____

3. _____

Recall the names of people you know who are facing ill health. Can you comfort these people in any of these same ways? Write the person's name or names below and what you will do to comfort that person.

Remember to thank God that He looks on your afflictions with compassion.

_____

_____

_____

DAY 2
What Is a Chemical Imbalance?

Purpose: To explain how depression can result from a chemical imbalance

Passage: Read Psalm 139 in preparation for today's study.

Created with a Body in Balance

David expressed amazement at God's full understanding of his every thought and action.

In Psalm 139 David expressed amazement that God has full understanding of his every thought and action. David's conclusion? *This is beyond me!*

> Such knowledge is too wonderful for me;
> It is too high, I cannot attain to it (Ps. 139:6).

Then David got even more personal. God didn't just know everything about David; God actually created David. Both David's inner being and outer frame were formed by God while in his mother's womb. This understanding motivated David to praise God for His astonishing work.

> For Thou didst form my inward parts;
> Thou didst weave me in my mother's womb.
> I will give thanks to Thee, for I am fearfully and wonderfully made;
> Wonderful are Thy works,
> And my soul knows it very well (Ps. 139:13-14).

Although each part of the body was intricately designed to work in a specific way, the fall created problems for us. When sin entered the world, it impacted the way all of our bodies' systems work.

The body's systems suddenly became subject to health problems. Those conditions include heart problems, lung disease, the lack of insulin production in diabetes, tendonitis, and muscular and skeletal problems to name a few. Some diseases such as cancer can lead to death, while other maladies cause temporary or long-term discomfort.

Since every system of the body can break down in some way, the brain is not exempt. Chemical imbalance may result from the brain's dysfunction.

What Is a Chemical Imbalance?

"I will give thanks to Thee, for I am fearfully and wonderfully made" (Ps. 139: 14).

Research has revealed that depressed individuals have lower levels of chemicals called neurotransmitters in the brain. In the case of depression, two of these chemicals are norepinephrine and serotonin.

The most prominent theory among researchers today is that increased stress over a prolonged period of time leads to a decrease in these neurotransmitters. While we do not know for certain how antidepressant medications operate, they have the effect of increasing either norepinephrine or serotonin, or both. The end result is a restoration of brain chemistry to its proper balance.

Some Christians argue that medications are rarely in God's will. However, the simple advice of the theologian and Bible teacher Lewis Sperry Chafer is helpful. In responding to the idea that medical remedies are against the will of God, Chafer responds that medicine "is usually the supply of elements needed in the system for its recovery. Hence to use remedies for healing is no different in principle than to feed the body with food or to clothe it for warmth."[1]

For a more complete explanation of neurotransmitters see *Happiness Is a Choice* by Frank Minirth, and Paul Meier. (Grand Rapids: Baker Books, 1978.)

Responding to Chemical Imbalance

If you find yourself depressed for no apparent reason—that is to say your depression seems unrelated to an event, circumstance, or person in your past or present—make an appointment with your medical doctor for an evaluation. He or she can help you determine if a chemical imbalance may be the cause or a contributor to your depression.

A person with a chemical imbalance will not recover from depression simply by trying harder, putting on a happy smile, staying busy, or praying more often. These represent words of advice from well-meaning friends who simply do not understand that the body needs help that can only be found through medical intervention. Seeking medical advice regarding depression is always an appropriate step to take. Even if seeing your doctor rules out physical causes, you will at least know that you explored this avenue and need to look further for the root of your depression.

We are a complex entity of mind, emotions, and body—all of which affect one another.

Should Christians Use Antidepressants?

Each Christian must answer this question individually after prayer and consultation with a physician and any other spiritual advisors the persons may feel led to approach. Although we cannot say antidepressants are right for you, we do feel strongly that they are not wrong for Christians in general.

The physical body does not work one way for Christians and another way for non-Christians. We are a complex entity of mind, emotions, and body—all of which affect one another. Antidepressants have been clinically proved to alleviate some of the troubling aspects of depression and in turn speed recovery and good mental and emotional health.

For example, inability to sleep is one of the signs of depression, although this condition may have other causes. Antidepressants facilitate sleep in most patients. Since good sleep can aid recovery—and poor sleep inhibits recovery—medically inducing sleep is often a worthy objective in treating depression.

Antidepressants should never be seen as a be-all-end-all treatment for depression. They should never be a long-term solution. However, in the short-term, elevating a person's mood can be an important ingredient in an over-all strategy for dealing with depression.

Spend some time thinking about your response to the issue of treating depression with medicine. If you have misgivings, discuss your feelings with your physician. Ask for pamphlets explaining chemical imbalance and the role of medicine in treating this condition. Discuss particular drugs you may have heard about through the media and/or those who have used these drugs. Remember: an informed Christian will make informed choices.

Close today's lesson in prayer. Thank God for your body. Thank Him for each part that is functioning correctly. Pray about any physical problems. Pray for others by name who you know are facing medical crises.

DAY 3
Stress and Overload

Purpose: To assess the level of stress in your life and causal factors

Passage: Read Philippians 4:6-7 in preparation for today's study.

A stress-filled life often causes a person to become discouraged or depressed. In the next three days of this week's study, we will explain how stress can result in depression and identify ways to live life in a more balanced manner.

What Is Stress?

Simply stated, stress is a person's response to overload, the accumulated effect of the pressures of life. Daily tasks, job-related duties, and volunteer projects may not appear staggering when viewed individually. But when they begin to layer one upon another, they can reach overwhelming proportions.

We actually need stress in God-managed proportions for normal growth and development.

We actually need stress in God-managed proportions for normal growth and development. Referred to as eustress from the Greek prefix meaning good, good stress motivates us to get our tasks accomplished. Often accompanied by an adrenaline flow, eustress provides the added "umph" or energy level for peak performance. The problems occur when we assume burdens and responsibilities which God did not plan for us. We take on more than God intended. When we accumulate too much stress, we move from eustress to distress.

The body was not designed to run on adrenaline all the time. Adrenaline "rush" is like passing gear in an automobile. When you press the accelerator pedal to the floor, the transmission shifts to a lower gear and the engine speeds up. The engine can produce more power at the higher speed, but if you drove in passing gear all the time, eventually you would burn out your engine!

We were created by our Heavenly Father with a limit on our capacity to carry stress. We can be overloaded with disastrous results. If we choose to consistently pile task upon task, the consequences are predictable: we will crash and burn! On the other hand, if we choose to run the marathon of life within our God-given limits, we will reach the finish line in good time by His grace.

Just what are your limits? Below list ways you feel overloaded.

_____

_____

_____

Overload is often a normal pattern for Americans. We may feel pressured to overload—or expect it. Sometimes we even take peculiar pride in how overloaded we've become. No wonder so many folks report feeling consistently tired and grumpy! Let's look at some areas in which we commonly misjudge our capacities.

Understanding Stress and Human Limitations

1. Time Limitations

How often have you planned a day filled with chores and activities, only to complete half of what you planned to do? When your time expectations are unrealistic, not even the best time-management system will help. We all have 24 hours a day to use; no more, no less.

Have you ever wished you could be the best parent, spouse, friend, coach, business owner or employee, Sunday School teacher, deacon, Bible study leader, and soul-winner—all at the same time? The truth is you never will be the best in all of these roles. You must choose a few areas in which to concentrate and invest your time wisely.

Have you ever wished you could be the best parent, spouse, friend, or employee all at the same time?

2. Physical Limitations

We all possess a limited amount of daily physical energy. Once we exhaust our allotted reserve, we must replenish through rest, exercise, and proper nutrition.

Experts report that our culture is plagued with "sleep-deprivation." What does that mean? It means Americans live their lives with too little rest. Rest is even more necessary for those experiencing discouragement or depression.

Following are some suggestions experts recommend for re-establishing regular sleep patterns.

1. Increase your sleep time by at least one hour. Some experts report that you need one hour more sleep than you think you need. For example, if you usually sleep for seven hours, you actually need to sleep for eight hours.

2. Practice a consistent bedtime routine. Establish a set bedtime each night, even on the weekends. After 7 p.m. refrain from eating high sugar content foods or drinking caffeine beverages.

3. Give your body opportunities to rest during the day. Consider a short nap. To prevent a draggy feeling, keep the nap less than 30 minutes. If you can't nap, set aside a few minutes to relax your mind. Listening to soft music is often helpful.

4. Plan your monthly calendar to include some relaxed weekends. Say no to any intense activities which threaten to invade those times. Scheduling requires work, but the physical and spiritual benefits are immeasurable.

Scheduling requires work, but the physical and spiritual benefits are immeasurable.

Beginning tonight, identify one step you will take to prepare for better sleep patterns.

Also our bodies warn us of physical limitations through pain. If we lift too heavy a weight, our bodies hurt. They cry out, "You overloaded me!" Likewise, if we ignore our bodies as they cry out for proper rest, diet, and exercise, we will likely experience physical symptoms of stress. All too often people attack life as if it is a sprint race. We can push ourselves for short periods of time, but not for weeks and months without physical consequences.

3. Relational Limitations

When we overload our lives with too many activities and responsibilities, key relationships tend to suffer. Family members may complain that we do not spend enough quality time at home. Spouses may feel threatened and unloved. Children may act out at school or church.

Stressful times tend to maximize irritability and minimize patience. As a rule relationship intimacy decreases as stress increases. Unfortunately, in our hurried lives we minimize the significance of relationships. Instead, we place value on accomplishment. Relationships need nurture and care. On Day 5 of this week's study we will look at setting priorities to ensure that those closest to us receive priority status.

4. Spiritual Limitations

Heightened stress affects our spiritual lives. Even though it is God's continual desire that we remain close to Him, in our overload we begin to limit the amount of time we spend with Him and in His Word. We neglect Him during the very time we most need Him.

When we feel distant from God and hopeless in our pursuit of Him, it may be time for a good night's sleep! Remember our study of Elijah in Week 1? When he became discouraged to the point of giving up, God ministered to him through food and rest. Then God ministered to Elijah by providing the spiritual encouragement he needed to fulfill his service to God.

The apostle Paul encouraged the Philippian Christians to draw on God's strength in this manner: "Be anxious for nothing, but in everything by prayer and supplication with thanksgiving let your requests be made known to God. And the peace of God, which surpasses all comprehension, shall guard your hearts and your minds in Christ Jesus" (Phil. 4:6-7). When the cares of life become too great, we need to take our concerns to God in prayer.

To manage our stress, we often need to begin with an objective look at our responsibilities. On a separate sheet of paper, list the hours in a day from the time you usually arise until the time you are usually asleep. Beside each hour, list what you would do on a typical weekday. Then, make separate lists for Saturday and Sunday. Fill in how you use your time, concentrating on activities you regularly accomplish. As you make your lists, consider personal care, family, work, church, social/volunteer activities, and free time or recreation. Analyze your list by answering the following questions:

1. Do I typically have built-in free time during each day?

2. Am I getting the amount of sleep I need to feel rested?

Stressful times tend to maximize irritability and minimize patience.

When the cares of life become too great, we need to take our concerns to God in prayer.

3. Is exercise a regular part of my week?

4. Have I made time for eating two to three balanced meals each day?

5. Do I enjoy regular time and activities with friends/loved ones?

6. Do I experience "times of refreshing" in my relationship with God, or is my relationship with God a source of guilt and shame?

7. As I look over my use of time, I would characterize my life as:
___balanced   ___unbalanced   ___somewhere in between

Every individual has a personal capacity for stress.

The time study above requires considerable work. Don't rush through it. An honest perspective of your stressors will help you develop a better managed lifestyle. We will address a plan for managing life in Day 5, "Balanced Living."

Conclude today's lesson by writing a note to God. Tell Him how you feel about the level of stress in your life. Ask Him to meet your specific need to manage life effectively.

_____

_____

_____

DAY 4
Stress and Medical Problems

Purpose: To explain how stress can lead to depression

Passage: Read John 15:4 in preparation for today's study.

Yesterday we defined *stress* as *the response to overload*. Not all stress is bad, and not all stressful experiences result in depression. However, too much stress in multiple areas (physical, mental, emotional, and spiritual), at one time, over an extended period of time can certainly lead to discouragement—if not depression. The formula may look like this.

Too much stress	+	Multiple areas of life	+	A long period of time	=	Discouragement and Depression

Every individual has a personal capacity for stress. One person may be able to deal with 10 pounds of mental stress, 15 pounds of physical stress, and 25 pounds of spiritual stress, while another's capacity may be only 25 pounds of mental, 10 pounds of physical stress, and 5 pounds of spiritual. God created each of us to be unique individuals. What may be extremely stressful for you may not affect another person at all. For example, a ride in a hot air balloon might be relaxing to you, but extremely stressful for a friend! Therefore, find your stress points. If you push your stress limit in multiple areas for long enough, discouragement and depression may result.

An Example of a Stressed Life

Sue recently married, moved to a new state, joined a new church, began a new job, and returned to college to finish her degree. The changes she faced are major stressors. For several weeks, all went reasonably well—until Sue began having some trouble sleeping. At first she ignored it, thinking it would go away, but it didn't.

Sue continued to trudge along until one day her mom called to say her dad was in intensive care due to a heart attack. Up to this point, Sue believed she was effectively balancing her multiple responsibilities, but her life began to change. She experienced problems with coworkers at her job. She slept even less, and her mind raced all the time. Her relationship with her husband was distant, her emotions unpredictable. Her relationship with God was marginal and even church was a chore. Sue was overloaded in too many areas. Do you think Sue is headed for an intense bout of discouragement or depression?

Learning from a Stressed Life

Several details from Sue's story can help us understand why her life began to take a negative turn. We can make two observations about Sue's experience.

First, Sue encountered some rather predictable stressors: new marriage, new job, new location, new studies, and new church. These changes were not unexpected; she had to plan each of them. Sue did not take into consideration the amount of stress she was deliberately heaping upon herself.

Sometimes we don't stop to consider the amount of stress we deliberately heap upon ourselves.

Second, Sue encountered one unexpected stressor: her dad's heart attack. This type of stress is unpredictable. She had no warning—it just happened. In Sue's case, it seemed to be the proverbial straw that broke the camel's back. Suddenly, Sue could no longer cope.

Relate an experience when you had at least two predictable stressors and then one or more unexpected stressors.

Predictable Stressors

1. _____

2. _____

Unexpected Stressors

1. _____

2. _____

Managing Life Stress

Sue did not allow for unexpected stressors. We frequently live as if we know the future. The truth is that only God knows what tomorrow has in store. In James 4:13-17, James instructed the merchant not to plan ahead as if next year's profit was a certainty. He provided this wise advice: "Instead, you ought to say, 'If the Lord wills, we will live and also do this or that' " (Jas. 4:15).

James reminds us that God should be in charge of our time. Since we know that unexpected stressors will come, we need to re-embrace our dependence on the Lord. John 15 describes Jesus as the vine and us as the branches. Branches totally depend on the vine for life and growth. Verse 4 says: " 'Abide in Me, and I in you. As the branch cannot bear fruit of itself, unless it abides in the vine, so neither can you unless you abide in Me.' "

Thus, the first lesson we learn about managing stress is to let God control our lives. Since we know He is not going to give us more to do than we have time for, we will not be in the quandary of overloading ourselves. A second lesson is to take responsibility for our choices. We think, *I can't do anything about these things; they are all forced on me.* In fact, we can and must take responsibility, not for evil things that happen to us, but for our own life management. A good word to remember is that while we often can do nothing about external circumstances, we are never completely powerless in how we respond to those circumstances.

We must manage the predictable stressors, but allow enough room in our lives for the unpredictable. Many times this balance comes as we grow older; it is what the Bible refers to as wisdom.

If you grew up in a family that successfully managed both types of stressors, you may have learned balance early. However, many persons are clueless about this concept until they experience an emotional or physical crash, at which point they realize they have mismanaged life.

While we often can do nothing about external circumstances, we are never completely powerless in how we respond to those circumstances.

Circle the areas below in which you need to be more dependent on God.

marriage	parenting	finances	school
friends	church	job	ministry
extended family	in-laws	leisure	health
past	future		

Take a moment and write below what you can do to deepen your dependency on God.

_____

_____

_____

_____

_____

The Role of Failed Expectations in Stress

Ed is the part-time minister of music in a medium-sized church. In January Ed announced to the choir that he had chosen an Easter pageant that would require excessive time and work. It also would cost more than the budgeted amount.

Without further explanation or discussion, Ed set a date for tryouts and began rehearsals one night a week. Soon the cast members were practicing twice a week, then three times a week. Ed drafted a construction crew of members to build the stage and set. A fund-raising committee worked to raise the needed money.

By the middle of February, the choir members were exhausted, the construction crew was complaining, and the fund-raising committee members were desperately calling church members for financial help. And believe it or not—everyone was mad at Ed!

Ed, in turn, was mad at the choir, the church, the pastor, and the janitor! No one was cooperating. Unfortunately, Ed didn't have a clue about what was happening. He never shared his expectations with the church. He never secured the church's commitment to such an extravagant performance. Ed felt unappreciated and misused. He didn't realize he'd done it to himself.

Many relational problems within the church family have to do with failed expectations. Persons with authority set themselves up for failure by expecting members to come through for them—usually without honestly stating their expectations on the front end. Then feelings are hurt on both sides and stress results.

Ed not only didn't communicate his expectations, but also he didn't allow others the dignity of choosing to be involved. Do you think his expectations were reasonable? ❏ yes ❏ no

Reflect on a recent experience when you felt someone let you down. Early on did you honestly and completely express your expectations? ❏ yes ❏ no

If not, how could stating expectations on the front end have helped the situation go more smoothly?

_____

_____

Let-Down Depression

Creative people frequently suffer from depression after completing a project.

Susan is an artist. Recently she experienced another type of stress-related depression. She completed a mural that required several months time. During those months Susan worked long hours. The project consumed her thoughts as well as her time. She looked forward to completion and enjoying some leisure time.

About a week after Susan finished the mural, she could hardly get out of bed in the mornings. She thought: *What is happening to me? I had all these plans. Now I can barely function.* Susan was suffering from another form of depression caused by stress. She was surprised to learn that creative people frequently suffer from depression after completing a project. Fortunately, Susan's depression lifted after a few weeks. Sometimes such depression lingers and becomes a greater problem.

Have you ever experienced depression after a major milestone or life accomplishment? ❑ yes ❑ no **If so, describe the experience.**

_____

_____

In tomorrow's study we will continue the discussion of stress management. We will provide some suggestions for ways to achieve balanced living.

DAY 5
Balanced Living

Purpose: To manage stress by implementing four keys to balanced living

Passage: Read Galatians 2:20 in preparation for today's study.

A tired-looking couple sat in our office one Tuesday afternoon. The look on their faces and the slump of their shoulders spoke volumes and indicated a constant "hurry up and go" lifestyle. They loved Jesus Christ and were active in their church; their marriage was solid and intimate; and their three school-aged children were happy and growing. So what was the problem? They just didn't see how they could maintain their hectic and busy lifestyle. They asked a simple and direct question: "Is it possible to have a balanced life?"

"Is it possible to have a balanced life?"

Our answer to them was equally simple and direct: "Truthfully, exact balance is rarely possible. But before you throw in the towel and walk away, let's consider a few principles for working toward balance."

First, You Can Live Without Experiencing Constant Stress.

Recall the definition of *stress: a person's response to overload, the accumulated effect of the pressures of life.* Keep in mind the following two points.

1. *Although God allows stressors into our lives, He does not choose for us a life of total stress.* We can respond to stressors in faith. In the words of David:

   From the end of the earth I call to Thee when my heart is faint;
   Lead me to the rock that is higher than I (Ps. 61:2).

Often a glance upward places the cares of life in proper perspective. We need to live in the assurance that we can go to a "rock that is higher than I." That assurance provides strength for the journey ahead.

Often a glance upward places the cares of life in proper perspective.

2. *Often burdens are the result of our own actions.* Whether our stressors are predictable or unexpected, we still can choose how we respond to them. For example, in Day 4, Sue could have chosen to wait a year or two to return to college. She would have had more time to settle into her new marriage, new location, new job, and new church. She would have enjoyed more time with her family, which would have allowed her to better accept the news of her father's heart attack.

Second, We Cannot Control All of Life's Many Variables.

Often stress results from our tendency and desire to control everything around us. Even when we take complete responsibility for every aspect of our lives, many factors remain out of our control. Consider the following analogy:

> A woman finally cleaned her house only to realize she had not been spending adequate time with the Lord. When she pursued and accomplished that goal, she realized that she really should be involved in friendships with other women. Once that area of life was back under control, she noticed her house was looking dirty again!

Our Lord sees the big picture, knows every contributing variable, and wants us to take comfort in His sovereign rule.

Does the story sound familiar? Control is not the mechanism we use to balance life. So many things are out of our control. To attempt to direct all of the events that affect and shape our lives is impossible and unrealistic, but Someone, our Lord, sees the big picture, knows every contributing variable, and wants us to take comfort in His sovereign rule.

> "Do not fear, for I am with you;
> Do not anxiously look about you, for I am your God.
> I will strengthen you, surely I will help you,
> Surely I will uphold you with My righteous right hand" (Isa. 41:10).

Remembering the above promises, let's turn our focus to the things over which you do have control as you seek to achieve and maintain balance in your life.

Third, Consider Four Keys to Balanced Living.

1. *Live by faith in Jesus Christ.* Take a look at the words of Paul to the church at Galatia. "I have been crucified with Christ; and it is no longer I who live, but Christ lives in me; and the life which I now live in the flesh I live by faith in the Son of God, who loved me, and delivered Himself up for me" (Gal. 2:20).

All attempts at balance ultimately flow from our connection with the hub of the universe—Jesus Christ. Three simple points in the verse above provide our first key to balanced living: "Since I have been crucified with Christ and Christ lives in me, I now live my life by faith in Him."

All attempts at balance ultimately flow from our connection with the hub of the universe—Jesus Christ.

Take a moment to read each of the following verses. Write in your own words how each one demonstrates the importance of exercising faith in Jesus as we seek to achieve balance in our lives.

Colossians 1:17 _____

_____

Colossians 2:6 _____

_____

Colossians 3:17 _____

_____

2. *Live by the Word of God.* The Bible provides keys for living a purposeful life. Bible reading and study keeps us from living life in an arbitrary "hit-or-miss" manner. Many mistakes and misjudgments that cause us stress could be prevented by following the examples of godly men and women in the Bible. The Bible also includes negative examples to show us what does and does not lead to healthy, balanced living. Scripture teaches principles for life management.

Unfortunately, some people approach the Bible in an almost magical fashion. They idealistically cling to the belief that if they read the Bible, somehow all the areas of their lives will fall into place and they will not experience stressors. Considering life's realities, the idea that we can live each day in perfect balance without problems is not a realistic goal.

If Bible study will not magically make my life more manageable, then how can it help? Reading God's Word provides opportunity for fellowship with the Author. It also reminds us to consistently apply those life principles the Bible teaches. James warned of persons who would hear the Word but not follow its teachings. Perfection is a destructive goal, but to live out the guidance Scripture supplies is both a constructive goal and a life-affirming habit.

Bible reading and study keeps us from living life in an arbitrary "hit-or-miss" manner.

> Thy word is a lamp to my feet
> And a light to my path (Ps. 119:105).

When are you best able to read your Bible?

❏ Early in the morning   ❏ At lunch time
❏ Before going to bed

Ask God to help you set aside time everyday for reading His Word and praying. Consider any person or activity that is standing in the way. Then ask the Father to help you prioritize His Word in your life.

3. *Live according to your priorities.* A balanced life requires priorities in keeping with the Word of God. *Priority* means *something that goes ahead of, or takes precedence over something else.* Consequently, when we refer to something as being first priority, we mean that it takes precedence over all that we do.

Priority does not mean a measure of time. We can make personal prayer and Bible study a priority, yet few of us are going to spend eight hours a day in quiet time. We should, however, plan to get eight hours of sleep. Priority means *this will get done, no matter what else has to go.*

Unfortunately, we all have experienced times when we neglect the most important matters in our lives and give attention to the trivial and unimportant issues. While seeking to schedule time and activities, we suggest the following order of priorities: time with God, time with family, time for work, time for ministry, and time for personal renewal.

A balanced life requires priorities in keeping with the Word of God.

Take a moment to evaluate the status of each time priority following. Are you currently neglecting any or several? Briefly describe the importance of each in your life.

Time with God _____

_____

Time with my family _____

_____

Time for work _____

_____

Time for ministry _____

_____

Time for personal renewal _____

_____

Goals represent specific plans we intend to carry out.

4. *Live your goals.* No person determines and arrives at the important priorities in life quickly or easily. We need to set specific goals that, when followed over a period of time, accomplish our life priorities (remember Day 4, Week 3?). Goals represent specific plans we intend to carry out. When setting individual goals or helping others to do so, remember the following three simple tests of a good goal.

- Brief enough to be remembered—Is my goal simple enough that I can discuss it with a friend without referring to notes?
- Specific enough to be written down—Can I write it down in one sentence?
- Clear enough to be achieved—Will I know when I've accomplished my goal? Is it measurable?

Consider and list two simple, specific, and clear goals for each of the priorities below. Remember, set goals that are achievable.

Time with God
Example: Each day I will read two chapters from the Bible.

1. _____

2. _____

Time with my family
Example: We will eat together during at least five family meals per week.

1. _____

2. _____

Time for work
Example: This month I will complete the Smith proposal.

1. _____

2. _____

Time for ministry
Example: I will call someone I know who needs encouragement.

1. _____

2. _____

Time for personal renewal
Example: I will exercise 20 minutes 3 times a week.

1. _____

2. _____

Live Intentionally

We will never achieve perfect control. We will never eliminate all problems or avoid all stressors. We can, however, do one thing to make an enormous difference in our lives. We have intended this unit to point you to that one thing: you can live intentionally rather than react to everything that happens around you. The work you have just completed is a starting place for living intentionally. Determining priorities and setting goals is the first step. Now, you must monitor those goals and keep moving imperfectly forward to achieve them.

Have you allowed yourself time to carefully and thoughtfully complete the assignments in this week? If so, congratulations. If, on the other hand, you have too many things to do, too much stress, too much pressure, we encourage you to give these simple steps a closer look. You can do it. By consistently following some priorities, under the lordship of Jesus, you can find relief from stress. Life can be not only manageable, but also joyful. Now that's a real hope!

Life can be not only manageable, but also joyful.

[1]Lewis Sperry Chafer, *Systematic Theology, Vol. VII* (Dallas: Dallas Seminary Press, 1948), 185.

Week 8

Poor Personal Choices: When My Sin Leaves Me Discouraged

Case in Point

Linda's father deserted the family when she was eight. Two years later her mother died. Linda and her younger sister were placed in an orphanage. "Someday," she consoled her sister, "Dad's going to come back for us." He never did. By age 29, Linda was filled with bitterness and anger. *Would anyone really love her if her own father did not?* she thought.

Cindy, Linda's friend at work, had also lived through a traumatic childhood, but she seemed at peace about her past. One day Cindy invited Linda to attend church with her on Sunday. Linda agreed, mostly out of curiosity. When the pastor began to speak, Linda heard the gospel message for the first time. At the end of his message she quietly walked forward, confessed her sin, and received Christ into her heart as Savior. Linda discovered a joy and a peace unlike anything she had ever before experienced.

Over the next few weeks Linda learned that she was responsible for her actions even if others had wronged her. She began to practice forgiveness toward those who had hurt her and to take responsibility for her own behavior. With the support of Cindy and other new church friends, Linda began to grow spiritually and emotionally.

This week you will ...
1. observe how poor choices can leave us discouraged;
2. learn to avoid the discouragement caused by reactions to the sins of others;
3. discover hope in the Lord's forgiveness while learning to forgive others.

What you'll study
Day 1: The Mercy of God
Day 2: Personal Choices
Day 3: Hope in the Lord's Forgiveness
Day 4: The Sins of Other People
Day 5: Forgiving Others

Memory verse
"I now rejoice, not that you were made sorrowful, but that you were made sorrowful to the point of repentance; for you were made sorrowful according to the will of God, in order that you might not suffer loss in anything through us" (2 Cor. 7:9).

DAY 1
The Mercy of God

Purpose: To affirm sadness when we sin as motivation from God for us to change

Passage: Read 2 Corinthians 7:8-13 in preparation for today's study.

To this point we have looked at four possible causes of discouragement and depression: loss (including grief and family of origin issues), anger, stress, and medical problems. This week we will study the fifth and final cause: poor choices—how our own sin and response to the sins of others can leave us discouraged or depressed.

Feelings of guilt, anger, shame, and despair caused by our own behavior are one of the great consequences of sin. God does not desire us to perpetually experience these feelings. He does allow them so we will adopt His attitude toward sin and pursue a life of obedient service to Christ.

In Genesis 4, Cain felt discouraged because God did not look with favor on his offering. God told him, " 'If you do what is right, will you not be accepted?' " (Gen. 4:7, NIV). God wanted Cain and the generations that followed him to understand from the beginning that their choices of whether to obey Him would have a definite impact on their feelings afterwards.

Our choices of whether or not to obey God have a definite impact on our feelings afterwards.

God's Mercy

God uses how we feel as a consequence of our sinful choices to make us more receptive to His free gift of eternal life in Jesus Christ. Once we are saved, He continues to use the painful feelings resulting from sin to direct us to a more obedient life. God's judgment on sin reflects His love and mercy. God does not want us to settle for anything less than a rich and meaningful life in Christ. Imagine what we would miss of peace and joy if He were lenient and indulging!

God does not want us to settle for anything less than a rich and meaningful life in Christ.

Our Repentance

Paul wrote the Corinthian Christians what he considered a very severe letter because he wanted them to experience the joy of obedient living. In the letter Paul encouraged them to forsake their complacent attitude toward the sinful behavior of one of their members.

Paul maintained that he did not regret any sorrow he had caused them by what he had written, because it was the type sorrow God intended—sorrow over sin. "Even if I caused you sorrow by my letter, I do not regret it. Though I did regret it—I see that my letter hurt you, but only for a little while—yet now I am happy, not because you were made sorry, but because your sorrow led you to repentance. For you became sorrowful as God intended and so were not harmed in any way by us. Godly sorrow brings repentance that leads to salvation and leaves no regret, but worldly sorrow brings death" (2 Cor. 7:8-10, NIV).

Paul was looking for the positive results that would later occur in the lives of the Corinthians. In this passage, he contrasted the discouragement God intends for our good and the discouragement He wants us to avoid.

The sorrow God desires produces repentance without regret; the sorrow of the world produces death. If the Corinthians had not responded to God, they would have remained in a discouraged and bitter state.

Clearly, the Lord is always working for our long-term benefit and contentment. While He may allow us to experience some discouragement to motivate corrections in our manner of living, God's ultimate goal is for us to experience joy.

The Lord is always working for our long-term benefit and contentment.

Our Hunger for God and Righteous Living

The person God motivates toward repentance can look forward to even more. Paul went on to say in 2 Corinthians 7:11-13 that sorrow according to the will of God produces a greater longing for righteous living.

Take a moment to list some of the positive things that sorrow produced in the lives of the Corinthians (2 Cor. 7:11-13).

1. _____

2. _____

3. _____

4. _____

5. _____

Describe a time in your life when "godly sorrow" worked for your benefit.

_____

_____

Discouragement and depression are not always rooted in sin. We have already considered four other causes: loss, anger, stress, and medical problems. However, this week's study highlights how poor personal choices affect emotional health. During the next three days we will examine how the Lord cares for us as a Father despite our sinful choices, how the sins of others affect us, and how to discover hope in God's forgiveness.

God allows us to experience sadness when we make poor choices in order to motivate us to change.

God continually displays His mercy in the lives of His children. Today we focused on one aspect of His mercy: He simply will not allow us to live happily in our sin. God allows us to experience sadness when we make poor choices in order to motivate us to change. His mercy and love lead us to a life of faith and obedience. Take a moment to thank God for His watch care over your life.

For Thou art my hope;
O Lord God, Thou art my confidence from my youth (Ps. 71:5).

DAY 2
Personal Choices

Purpose: To explain how personal sin can leave us discouraged

Passage: Read Psalm 32 in preparation for today's study.

God gave us the capacity to chart our own course in life. The decisions we make, good or bad, have consequences. Today we want to examine how poor personal choices affect our feelings—how personal sin can leave us discouraged.

In Psalm 32, David recounted his misery when he refused to respond to God. He pointed us to the happiness we find when we are open to the counsel of the Lord as He rebukes our sinful choices. From his own experience, David demonstrated how God's lovingkindness surrounds the one who listens to divine instruction.

David is an example of how God's lovingkindness surrounds the one who listens to divine instruction.

The Joy of Being Forgiven

David began by expressing the happiness and contentment a person experiences when God removes his or her sins.

> How blessed is he whose transgression is forgiven,
> Whose sin is covered! (Ps 32:1-2).

For a time, sinless perfection existed in the garden of Eden. Later, in the form of Jesus, perfection walked the earth, but we will not know perfection again until we reach heaven. Therefore, confession of sins is always necessary. John said, "If we say that we have no sin, we are deceiving ourselves, and the truth is not in us" (1 John 1:8). To deny personal sin is to escape reality, but each one of us can find the blessing of which David spoke. The New Testament promises, "If we confess our sins, He is faithful and righteous to forgive us our sins and to cleanse us from all unrighteousness" (1 John 1:8-9).

How often do you take time to confess your sin?

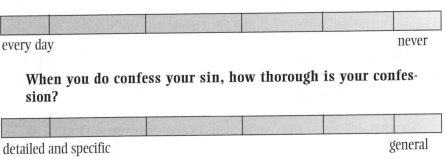

every day   never

When you do confess your sin, how thorough is your confession?

detailed and specific   general

The Father's Discipline

God disciplines His children because He is the ultimate good parent. Sometimes discipline purposes to bring the child to the point of confession and repentance. Sometimes discipline serves to train us in obedient living.

God disciplines His children because He is the ultimate good parent.

The following is a description of David's experience with God the Father's discipline. Underline any of David's words that might also describe an experience you've had with God's discipline.

> When I kept silent about my sin, my body wasted away
> Through my groaning all day long.
> For day and night Thy hand was heavy upon me;
> My vitality was drained away as with the fever heat of summer
> (Ps. 32:3-4).

When did your experience of God's discipline occur?

_____

How long did it last?

_____

David described the misery he brought on himself. As we learned in yesterday's study, God's judgment was actually mercy because it led David to confess his sins and ask for forgiveness.

Confession and Forgiveness

David shared his experience of confession and forgiveness and then encouraged all of us to do likewise.

> I acknowledged my sin to Thee,
> And my iniquity I did not hide;
> I said, "I will confess my transgressions to the Lord,"
> And Thou didst forgive the guilt of my sin.
> Therefore, let everyone who is godly pray to Thee. …
> Thou dost surround me with songs of deliverance (Ps. 32:5-7).

In a 180-degree turn from his former misery and deep discouragement, David discovered joy. The simple act of agreeing with God that he had unconfessed sin coupled with his willingness to confess filled David with joy.

Faith is essential to an effective walk with God.

In both the Old and New Testaments we learn that faith is essential to an effective walk with God. A key element of faith concerns confession. Faith means we believe God when He promises to forgive our sin. We know that God has forgiven us—not by our feelings, not by circumstances, but by faith.

To what degree do you accept or recognize that you are forgiven?

❑ I believe and accept God's forgiveness.
❑ I sometimes wonder if I am truly forgiven.
❑ I still think I have to make up for my sins myself.
❑ I don't believe God could forgive my sins.
❑ Though I want to, I have a difficult time believing God has forgiven me.

❑ Other _____

Be Teachable

We don't have to live our lives burdened by the misery of unconfessed sin. God promised to instruct, teach, and counsel us in the way we should go (see Ps. 32:8). David concluded by warning us to be quick to hear, unlike a horse or mule that requires a bit and bridle to stimulate obedience (see Ps. 32:9).

We tend to be slow learners by nature! If we were truly honest with ourselves, we would admit we often resemble cranky mules with bits in our mouths! But God in His mercy and love wants to remove the bits from our mouths. He desires to replace it with a willing heart. This process takes time. Salvation occurs when we trust Christ alone for our salvation—it is immediate and conclusive. Growth, on the other hand, is a process that continues during the daily course of our lives.

We tend to be slow learners by nature!

This study centers on one aspect of the growth process—the discovery of hope. If your discouragement or depression is the result of unconfessed sin, why not follow David's example:

Many are the sorrows of the wicked;
But he who trusts in the Lord, lovingkindness shall surround him (Ps. 32:10).

Take a moment and ask God to reveal the areas where you have fallen short, then record what He reveals to you.

_____

_____

_____

Now, ask God for His forgiveness based on the payment Christ has made in our place. Thank God for His forgiveness and ask Him to teach you and counsel you today, specifically in the situations you listed. By faith believe His promise of forgiveness.

As far as the east is from the west,
So far has He removed our transgressions from us (Ps. 103:12).

DAY 3
Hope in the Lord's Forgiveness

Purpose: To experience more fully the love of God the Father and the joy He has in forgiving us

Passage: Read Luke 15:11-24 in preparation for today's study.

God's willingness to forgive is one of the most difficult teachings of Scripture. Forgiveness contradicts our idea of fairness because justice assumes the guilty person should be punished—or at least demonstrate rehabilitation before we forgive.

The prodigal son appears to have used the natural line of reasoning about punishment. Imagine his thoughts as he fed the swine, "I will get up and go to my father, and will say to him, 'Father, I have sinned against heaven, and in your sight; I am no longer worthy to be called your son; make me as one of your hired men' " (Luke 15:18-19). He could no longer imagine himself as a son enjoying a close relationship with his father. You remember the rest of the story. The father's love surpassed his expectations. The prodigal son discovered that life is not about fairness but his willingness to recognize his own sin and humbly approach the Father.

Life is not about fairness but our willingness to recognize our own sin and humbly approach the Father.

This is the simple message of the gospel:
- We have sinned: "All have sinned and fall short of the glory of God" (Rom. 3:23).
- God offers grace: "Being justified as a gift by His grace through the redemption which is in Christ Jesus" (Rom. 3:24).
- We must believe: "If you confess with your mouth Jesus as Lord, and believe in your heart that God raised Him from the dead, you shall be saved" (Rom. 10:9).

The Love of the Father

Now, let's look at the father's reaction in the same story. Those who know Jesus as personal Savior have difficulty understanding God's unconditional love and the joy He feels in forgiving His children. Grace is so overwhelming. Here's a stunning illustration of that difficult-to-grasp grace of God. " 'But while he was still a long way off, his father saw him, and felt compassion for him, and ran and embraced him, and kissed him' " (Luke 15:20).

Are you surprised that the father had been waiting for his son? Take a moment to identify and list the father's loving actions (Luke 15:20-24).

1. _____

2. _____

3. _____

4. _____

5. _____

The son had been gone a long time. Probably the father had left his house and peered down the road many times to see if his son was coming home. He was deeply concerned about the son's welfare, and perhaps had asked travelers if they had any news of his whereabouts. The son, not being a father, did not realize that most parents never forget about their children.

The father was moved by the sight of his son with torn and disheveled clothes. The once proud young man was now broken and humiliated. Notice the father's response: he "felt compassion … ran and embraced him … kissed him."

The Heavenly Father is always waiting to embrace us if we simply turn to Him in faith—guaranteed.

In this story, Jesus drew a word picture illustrating the Heavenly Father's love for us. He is always waiting to embrace us if we simply turn to Him in faith—

guaranteed. Because of our own sin and shame, we tend to expect punishment. We may even fear we have severed and destroyed our relationship with the Father, but that is only our perspective. He will never abandon His relationship with us. God's response is always compassion and a loving embrace for the one who comes to Him in humble repentance.

The Joy of the Father

This story contains more than just the love of the Father, as important as that is. There is joy in forgiveness. The prodigal son did not expect a loving reception. He merely hoped to be accepted as a slave. The father, however, exceeds the son's wildest dreams and showers him with gifts to demonstrate love, forgiveness, and joy at his son's return home. " 'The father said to his slaves, "Quickly bring out the best robe and put it on him, and put a ring on his hand and sandals on his feet; and bring the fattened calf, kill it, and let us eat and be merry" ' " (Luke 15:22-23).

The second surprise in the story is the giving of gifts to the son. Describe three ways your Heavenly Father has blessed you beyond your expectations when you knew you deserved less.

1. _____

2. _____

3. _____

When the father observed his son's condition, he immediately clothed him in his best robe, placed a ring on his hand, and sandals on his feet. He ordered a joyful feast to celebrate his return. Just as Jesus had explained earlier to His disciples using the parables of the lost sheep and lost coin, when one sinner repents, "there is joy in the presence of the angels of God" (Luke 15:10). When the son returned home, there was joy in the presence of the father.

Take a moment to imagine the joy in heaven when you repented and returned to the Heavenly Father. If you have unconfessed sin in your life, stop and repent right now. Say to the Father, "I have sinned against heaven and in your sight." Then take time to enjoy the Lord's forgiveness as the Father wraps a fine robe around you, places a ring on your finger, and puts sandals on your feet.

Take a moment to imagine the joy in heaven when you repented and returned to the Heavenly Father.

DAY 4
The Sins of Other People

Purpose: To determine to respond to the sins of other people in such a way that we do not become discouraged

Passage: Read Genesis 50:15-21 in preparation for today's study.

Other people's sins often affect us in negative ways because their words and actions influence us. The familiar saying, "Sticks and stones may break my bones, but words will never hurt me" was never true. Although words cannot physically cut and bruise, they inflict pain in far deeper ways.

Today we will focus on ways to respond to the sins of others to prevent their behavior from causing us to become discouraged. And, if you already are suffering depression as a result of another's actions in the past, we'll look at ways to find hope and healing in the Lord.

Joseph continued to see God above and beyond the unkind acts of others.

Perhaps Joseph is the best example of someone who continued to see God above and beyond the unkind acts of others. His words in Genesis 50:20 to the brothers who sold him into slavery demonstrated his spiritual understanding. He had the ability to see God at work amidst his troubled circumstances. "As for you, you meant evil against me, but God meant it for good in order to bring about this present result, to preserve many people alive."

Let's divide the verse into three parts and highlight God at work in our lives:

1. Their plan: you meant evil against me;
2. God's plan: but God meant it for good;
3. God's purpose: in order to bring about this present result.

You Meant Evil Against Me

Personal healing and growth require us to view life in a realistic manner. We must take an honest look at both ourselves and the world around us to draw conclusions based on how things actually are rather than how we would like them to be. The life of Christ illustrates this point. Early in the Gospel of John, we read that "many believed in His name, beholding His signs which He was doing. But Jesus, on His part, was not entrusting Himself to them, for He knew all men" (John 2:23-24). Jesus kept a realistic perspective as He walked among men. He knew what people were capable of, and while this knowledge did not stop Him from loving them, it did cause Him to walk wisely.

Sometimes others actually do intend evil against us. Joseph experienced such evil when his brothers sold him into slavery. Years later, standing face-to-face with them, Joseph responded from a realistic viewpoint, "You meant evil against me." The statement was, of course, true. The reality of the situation could not and should not be rationalized.

We cannot really grade degrees of evil behavior because all evil hurts both God and other people.

We cannot really grade degrees of evil behavior because all evil hurts both God and other people. Yet think about the evil committed by Joseph's brothers. They tried to kill him, then instead sold him as a slave. On the scale below mark the degree of evil you consider their actions.

moderately evil   extremely evil

On the same scale above, mark the spot indicating the most serious evil anyone has committed against you.

We do not intend the last activity to either minimize or exaggerate the hurt you have experienced. Instead, we want to identify two truths. First, we need to objectively recognize the full seriousness of an offense. Second, we need to destroy the illusion of uniqueness. No matter how extreme the offenses we have suffered, others have suffered similar or worse treatment. We all share in the human condition. We have sinned and hurt others. Others have sinned and hurt us.

We have sinned and hurt others. Others have sinned and hurt us.

Sometimes others inflict harm through thoughtlessness or unintentional neglect. If we immediately interpret these instances as deliberate offenses against us and wrongly assume others have evil motives, we make ourselves vulnerable to unnecessary and pointless pain.

When you are uncertain as to whether the hurtful actions of others are intentional, ask yourself the following questions:

1. Have I ever known this person to act this way before? (Is this action characteristic of him or her?)

2. Do I know this person's current circumstances? (Perhaps they are experiencing some difficulty or crisis.)

3. Have I stopped to pray about the situation? (Am I missing something only God can see?)

But God Meant It for Good

God's hand is at work in our lives whether or not others intend to cause us pain. Seeing God at work was not easy for someone being sold into slavery—or later thrown into prison, innocent of any crime. When Joseph eventually disclosed his identity to his brothers, he could not contain his deep emotions and "wept so loudly that the Egyptians heard it" (Gen. 45:2). Why? Because through the years Joseph had been sustained by his ability to understand that his difficulties were not simply the result of his brothers' cruelty or Potiphar's injustice. Joseph believed God is truly "the ruler of the kings of the world" (Rev. 1:5). Paul reflects this same belief in Romans 8:28, "We know that God causes all things to work together for good to those who love God, to those who are called according to His purpose."

Recall a time when someone purposely hurt you. How has God worked that circumstance for good in your life?

_____

_____

_____

To Bring About This Present Result

God knew that to keep His people alive during seven long years of famine He would have to sustain them in Egypt. Only God knows the future, and only He can be trusted to prepare us for it.

Only God knows the future, and only He can be trusted to prepare us for it.

Perhaps you have suffered through some very difficult experiences. Only God knows His purpose and plan for you. We cannot possibly grasp all that He intends and desires. However, we can trust Him to use the evil plans of others for good in our lives. The wrong intentions of other people may sometimes shake our hope in Jesus Christ, but they cannot shake our Hope—Jesus Christ.

DAY 5
Forgiving Others

Purpose: To forgive others even when their actions have caused deep hurt

Passage: Read Matthew 6:12 in preparation for today's study.

This week we have examined how our personal choices can leave us discouraged and depressed. Here's a brief review.

1. Day 1: The Mercy of God—God allows us to experience sadness when we sin to motivate us to change.

2. Day 2: Personal Choices—Our poor personal choices affect how we feel. In Psalm 32 David described the misery he felt when he refused to respond to God. He pointed out the happiness we can experience by being open to the Lord's counsel when He rebukes our sinful choices.

3. Day 3: Hope in the Lord's Forgiveness—The story of the prodigal son revealed the love of God the Father and the joy He has in forgiving us.

4. Day 4: The Sins of Other People—We can respond to the sins of others in ways that prevent discouragement. For example, Joseph was able to see God above and beyond the unkind acts of others.

Will I Ever Forget?

Many Christians struggle with forgiveness. Tom was wronged by his former business partner Mark. His heart ached as he remembered how Mark manipulated him out of several thousand dollars and marred his reputation. He tried to put the incident out of his mind, but it was no use. At one point he was gripped by a surge of pain and anger that seemed to consume his whole body. Later, Tom asked the Lord to help him because, in his own strength, he was unable to forgive Mark and lay his anger to rest.

Shouldn't we be able to forget when we have forgiven someone?

What happened to Tom? How can a Christian forgive, yet still be plagued with negative feelings? Shouldn't we be able to forget when we have forgiven someone? When Jesus taught the disciples to pray, He said, " 'Forgive us our debts, as we also have forgiven our debtors' " (Matt. 6:12). Clearly forgiveness is not optional for a Christian. We must not harbor anger; we need God's grace in our daily struggles to forgive those who have offended us.

We need to distinguish between forgiving and feeling. Forgiving is a choice, an act of the will. Feelings occur largely outside our immediate control. Forgiveness does not assure that we no longer experience negative feelings. Look again at Matthew 6. When Jesus taught the disciples to pray, He did not instruct them to pray only once for food, or once for temptations and deliverance from evil. Forgiveness requires daily attention.

What about situations like Tom's? Mark had indeed wronged him, affecting both his financial security and his business reputation. His problem could also be compounded by other painful situations from his past. Often we continue to carry around strong emotional memories of abuse, neglect, and mistreatment.

Forgiving starts with a choice, but it often must continue with a grief process. In Tom's case, he lost a friend, finances, and reputation. The experience damaged his trust in others and his confidence in his abilities. Tom will never fully forget the experience. However, by going through the same grief process we studied earlier, he will be able to put the loss behind him.

Forgiving starts with a choice.

Grieving Our Losses

In week 3, "Loss: Grieving Significant Losses," we learned that people can and do move beyond their losses—but it is a process. At the final stage, when we accept the loss, we begin to develop new hopes and goals.

For Tom to truly forgive Mark, he must enter the acceptance stage. Let's review the three key components to acceptance:

- believing that God has plans for your future;
- being willing to make a life for yourself; and
- setting new goals.

Regarding forgiveness, acceptance means *letting go.* You can let go of negative memories when you can believe God has positive plans for your future. The pain and wrongs caused by others' actions will diminish as you are willing to make a life for yourself and set new goals.

You can let go of negative memories when you can believe God has positive plans for your future.

Tom wrestled with his emotions for a while. As he daily sought to forgive Mark in accordance with Matthew 6:12, he began to believe that God did have plans for his future. He set a goal to restore his business reputation within the community. He looked to God for strength and changed his "what if" attitude to an attitude which demonstrated, "I can do all things through [Christ] who strengthens me" (Phil. 4:13).

List the name(s) of a person or persons that you find it difficult to forgive.

_____

_____

_____

_____

_____

Do you believe that God has plans for your future? ❑ Yes ❑ No

Are you willing to make a life for yourself? ❑ Yes ❑ No

Identify and list two or three new goals for yourself. Remember, make your goal statements brief enough to be remembered, specific enough to be written down, and clear enough to be achieved.

_____

_____

_____

_____

_____

Close out your week's study with two actions. First, pray about the goal statements you have written. Ask God for His strength, guidance, and wisdom as you seek to accomplish these aims. Then copy your goals on a card to carry in your pocket or purse. Review the goals regularly. Pray about them. Ask God's help daily as you work to forgive.

Week 9

Hope for Today!

Case in Point

Laura felt anxious waiting for her first appointment with the orthodontist. No longer would she have to look at those ugly crooked teeth. After today she would be a beauty queen. At least that's what Laura told herself.

The dentist met with Laura and her mom for about 30 minutes while answering all their questions. He was thorough and caring. Both Laura and her mom were pleased.

Well, Laura was pleased until the doctor told her how long it would take for her teeth to achieve movie-star status. Yes, she heard him correctly—three years! It sounded like an eternity to her. She had expected it to take about six months. Nor was Laura prepared for all the changes involved. She had to eliminate certain foods. She would have to undergo regular, painful periods of tightening and adjusting the braces. And, of course, she could not overlook the possible teasing from others about her new "wiry" smile. So much for a short and simple process.

Laura illustrates a typical American mentality toward health and healing. We want it, and we want it now! The healing process required for discouragement and depression is neither short nor simple. It will probably take longer than you thought and require more work than you expected. But let us tell you firsthand—it's worth it!

This week you will …
- learn the importance of admitting you can't do it alone;
- understand specific steps to change;
- practice being still and resting in Christ;
- learn to cultivate friendships that will heal.

What you'll study
Day 1: A Model of Change from the Bible
Day 2: An Experience with Depression
Day 3: Give Up Your Expectations
Day 4: Find an Encourager!
Day 5: Jesus Invites You to Come

Memory verses
"If we hope for what we do not see, we eagerly wait for it with perseverance. Likewise the Spirit also helps in our weaknesses. For we do not know what we should pray for as we ought, but the Spirit Himself makes intercession for us with groanings which cannot be uttered" (Rom. 8:25-26, NKJV).

DAY 1
A Model of Change from the Bible

Purpose: To explain a four-stage change process

Passage: Read Acts 10 in preparation for today's study.

We have studied discouragement and depression. We have considered five common causes. Now we need to ask the practical question: How do I make the changes necessary to recover?

The Bible contains principles and strategies for growth and change.

We have good news. Just as the Bible points us to heaven, it also shows the way here on earth. It contains principles and strategies for growth and change. Today's study presents one model of change found in the Bible that can be applied to discouragement and depression. Read Acts chapter 10 to observe the model as it was played out in the life of the apostle Peter.

Stage 1: Awareness

Often change begins when God suggests a new and specific direction for us.

Often change begins when God suggests a new and specific direction for us to go. He can speak either softly or boldly. Verses 10-16 record Peter's experience with stage one, awareness.

Peter watched as a large sheet descended to earth. A variety of animals filled the sheet (see vv. 11-12). God told Peter to kill and eat, but Peter responded to God with an emphatic *no!* His was not a particularly uncommon response to God when He asks us to do something outside our comfort zone, especially when He breaks through our thin veneer of self-protection.

> **While studying *Strength for the Journey*, has God heightened your awareness of certain areas of your life that require change? List those areas of awareness below.**

_____

_____

_____

_____

Notice Peter's response to this new awareness from God. He resists—not once, not twice, but three times. Peter told God, *no!* Why did he resist so strongly? Because, according to his view of the world, good people did not eat unclean animals. Peter had observed the Jewish dietary laws all his life.

Sometimes when God creates a new awareness for us, it challenges ideas we have held dear all our lives. The most natural response to this stage is denial. Denial is an attempt on our part to erase the awareness God has provided. As a form of self-defense, we pretend that we have not heard what we heard, seen what we saw, or learned what we have come to understand.

Consider the statements below. Do any reflect an awareness God may be using to help you manage discouragement and depression? Check the ones that apply to you.

❑ You are too defensive.   ❑ You are too busy.

❑ Your priorities are confused.   ❑ You may need medical help.

❑ You need more time alone with God.   ❑ You need to rest more.

❑ Your friendships are superficial.   ❑ You get angry too easily.

❑ You continue to feel angry about events from your childhood.

Describe any additional awareness not on the list above that God has impressed on you.

_____

_____

Things to remember about awareness in this stage:

1. The solution may seem unusual, foreign, or even repulsive.
2. Awareness may take time to develop (for Peter it took at least three times).
3. We may need confirmation from God that the awareness is from Him.
4. We may automatically deny the truth.

Awareness make take time to develop.

Stage 2: Understanding

We enter the second stage when we move from denial to understanding. In this stage we fully accept our new awareness from God as truth! We conquer the struggle when we say, "Yes, I accept the fact that God has revealed this to me."

Peter first voiced understanding when he referred to the vision given to him earlier by God about the unclean animals. He said to Cornelius, "God has shown me that I should not call any man common or unclean" (Acts 10:28, NKJV). The second time Peter revealed his newfound understanding appears later in the same chapter: "Then Peter opened his mouth and said: 'In truth I perceive that God shows no partiality. But in every nation whoever fears Him and works righteousness is accepted by Him' " (Acts 10:34-35, NKJV).

Pam had been ill with a heart condition for two years. During that time she could hardly walk from one room to the next. Her doctor told her he believed she was depressed and that her depression was adding to her heart condition. Pam finally confronted her denial and began to move to stage two when she heard herself saying: "I am not depressed. I just cry all the time." Like Peter's realization that God cared for all people, Pam recognized she needed to deal with her depression.

The stage two question for us is, "I understand what God has revealed to me and I accept it, but what's next?" Now you're ready for stage three: taking the first steps toward new behavior.

We enter the second stage when we move from denial to understanding.

Stage 3: Action

Peter preached the gospel to Cornelius and those gathered at his home (see vv. 36-43). To the amazement of all, the Holy Spirit fell on the Gentiles and Peter baptized them (see vv. 44-48).

A person does not have to possess complete awareness and understanding before acting. Remember, Peter accompanied the messengers from Cornelius before he fully understood what God wanted him to do.

We could refer to the action stage as "learning to walk."

We could refer to this stage as "learning to walk." We attempt a new behavior, but in the beginning we are very likely to fail. This potential failure is only an indication that we are attempting to accomplish a new task, one we've never tried before. It's much like the child who goes from training wheels to no training wheels. As fathers, we have been privileged to run alongside our children riding bikes, holding tightly to the seat as they learned to balance this new two-wheeled experience. Our kids never—we repeat never—pedaled off successfully the first time. Why? Because it was a new behavior, a new skill.

Any change in life works the same way. The first few attempts are awkward and rarely successful. But that's OK. The point is that by God's grace you are "trying out" new ways to live your life.

What new actions can you take now to help deal with discouragement and depression? List three actions below. Then record the date you put the behavior into practice. For possible actions, consider the five causes of depression. What can you do to reduce stress? What can you do to address medical problems? etc.

ACTION	DATE
1._____	_____
2._____	_____
3._____	_____

Stage 4: Change

Change itself is a culmination of the three previous stages.

Change itself is the final stage of the change process and is a culmination of the three previous stages. At this point we begin to live more of our life with the new behavior in place than without it.

For example, suppose a person believed God wanted him to exercise three times a week. Change would be effective when he or she consistently practiced the behavior for 40 out of 52 weeks each year, or most of the time.

Change does not mean perfection. It means living out more of the new behavior than the old. Change in Peter's life occurred when he accepted that God desired to offer salvation to the Gentiles as well as to the Jews. Peter maintained this change by contending with those who insisted on circumcision in Acts 11:2. He argued that God would save those outside of Israel if they would accept His Son Jesus. Again at the Jerusalem Council in Acts 15: 7-11, Peter voiced the change he experienced by stating that God wanted to save the Gentiles.

Peter remained consistent with this change until the incident related in Galatians 2:11-14 when he gave in to social pressure. He accommodated those who believed Gentiles should be circumcised and follow Jewish law. Paul confronted him about this inconsistency. Peter clearly had changed, but the change was not perfection. People frequently regress to former behavior.

Where do you see yourself in the biblical change process related to discouragement or depression? Circle your present stage or circle between the stages if that better describes where you are in the process.

Where are you in the change process?

Awareness	Understanding	Action	Change

Explain why you believe you are at that particular point in the process. What is necessary for you to continue the change process? Write your response below.

_____

_____

_____

God offers us hope by providing a strategy that leads to lasting change.

God offers us hope by providing a strategy that leads to lasting change.

DAY 2
An Experience with Depression

Purpose: To illustrate the biblical change process as it applies to discouragement and depression

Passage: Read John 15:5 in preparation for today's study.

We have a friend who experienced serious depression. Take a look at how he applied the biblical change process we studied in day 1. Our prayer is that this process will guide you on your own journey.

Stage 1: Awareness

Matt never thought he would personally experience depression. God did a lot of work to bring him to an awareness of his own needs and limits. Matt became aware of the following situations during his depression.

1. *Physical limits.* Matt's depression had a definite onset. One day as he arrived home, Matt felt uneasy and anxious. While talking with his wife, he began to feel as if he were pressured by a huge weight and something *broke* inside him. His body gave him a clear message that he was physically overloaded and had been for several years. Matt began to experience insomnia as well as massive loss of appetite, losing nearly 15 pounds in less than 10 days.

Matt never admitted that he "could not" do a task. He was a self-made man and believed that with a little time and effort, he could accomplish anything. Yet now he was forced to admit that he felt totally empty and unable to function. He felt as if his life was shattered. For the first time Matt experientially agreed with Jesus, "Apart from me you can do nothing" (John 15:5, NIV).

2. *Lack of rest.* Matt continued his frantic work pace, not realizing he was a workaholic. His rationalization was that he was merely a good family provider who loved the Lord. He thought he was being lazy to take time out for rest. Later Matt would see the benefit of taking a nap or going to bed early.

3. *Need for others.* Matt's wife Sandy provided tremendous emotional and spiritual support, as did several friends God strategically placed in his life. Not all of them understood what he was going through, but they all genuinely loved and supported him. Finally Matt humbled himself, admitted that his life was out of control, and asked for help. This help eventually included his family doctor and a professional counselor.

Stage 2: Understanding

It took Matt several months to accept all the pieces of awareness we just identified. He resisted, hoping his depression would end or get better on its own, but it did not. Finally he said, "I hurt so badly, I'll do whatever it takes to get well." Matt accepted that he was clinically depressed and unable to help himself by himself. However, several emotions hindered him from immediately entering the understanding phase.

1. Fear of rejection: Matt feared what people would say when he admitted that he, a manager in a major company, was depressed.

2. Fear of failure: For Matt to admit that he was depressed meant to admit that he could not do life "perfectly." Anything less than perfection was unacceptable for Matt. The depression shattered his whole image of the perfect Christian and replaced it with the image of a broken Christian.

3. Hopelessness: Matt mistakenly thought that if he accepted his depression, he might never recover. His motto was "Better to deny than to die." Even still, his hopeless thoughts horrified him. While Matt now knows that he was never beyond hope, things certainly felt hopeless at the time.

Piece by piece Matt turned loose of his fear and hopelessness. Gradually he moved from awareness to understanding.

Stage 3: Actions

Matt began to take specific actions essential to conquering his depression. Some of these actions included the following:

1. *He admitted his depression to others.* Matt did not broadcast his condition to everyone he met, but he was open with those closest to him and others who

needed to know. He learned he did not possess the energy during the depression to "fake" happiness or joy. He realized that masking his true experience was more damaging in the long run than the exposure and potential rejection openness invited.

2. *He developed a family plan.* Matt and his wife formed a plan to keep the home routine normal despite his anxiety and stress. They talked daily about his progress and she prayed for him. They didn't hide his depression from their children nor did they give the children graphic details of his emotional plight.

3. *He enlisted support.* Matt met weekly with good friends for spiritual refreshment and encouragement. At times he felt as though he lived only to see them and hear them say they believed God could and would bring him through his present discouragement. Knowing that his friends continued to pray for him helped Matt enormously.

4. *He sought professional help.* At the recommendation of Matt's family physician, Matt located a reputable Christian counselor who helped him initiate the healing process.

6. *Matt never gave up hope!* He learned to keep hoping even in his darkest moments and days. Matt discovered he could lose all sense of his Heavenly Father during this difficult time. Not being able to feel God's presence was painful. Yet, even on the worst days, the Father empowered him to "hang on."

Stage 4: Change

A teacher in graduate school said this to the class: "If you want something to change, then you must change something." If you are in the overpowering grip of discouragement or depression, passivity will be your worst enemy. Be proactive. Act and watch our Lord work in your life by providing hope.

Our friend Matt is still changing. He has come a long way, but he still has a long way to go. Over the past years he has experienced substantial change in several areas of his life.

"If you want something to change, then you must change something."

1. He has a relationship to God. For the first time in Matt's life, he feels accepted by the Heavenly Father. No longer is he paralyzed for long periods of time by guilt and shame. Matt's life is a testimony to God's grace.

2. He now tolerates personal failure. Matt seeks to accept the act of admitting failure as the avenue to knowing God better. He is searching to know more about the truth found in Jesus' words, "Apart from Me you can do nothing."

3. He practices transparency and honesty. The need to hide who he really is or to project a super "ideal" self has greatly diminished. Matt has learned that his past pain gives him access to people. Being who he is frees him to do the work the Father has called him to do.

4. He is more tolerant of the failures of others. Matt's brokenness has given him compassion for the wounded. The God of all comfort comforted him so that he might in turn comfort others.

5. His passion for people increased. Now that he understands Jesus can repair broken lives, Matt feels free to care for and minister to people. His desire for intimacy with others has increased. He spends more time with his wife. He wants a closer relationship with friends who share his love for Jesus Christ.

6. He possesses a stronger sense of hope. Even in dark days, Matt knows that God is faithful and will protect and guide his life.

God is faithful and will protect and guide our lives.

Review Matt's six action steps and the six changes Matt experienced as he dealt with his depression. Circle any ideas you need to incorporate into your growth plan.

How is Matt's story similar to your own?

_____

_____

_____

How is it different?

_____

_____

_____

DAY 3
Give Up Your Expectations!

Purpose: To develop openness to God's plans for how you will be healed

Passage: Read 2 Kings 5:1-15 in preparation for today's study.

A Desperate Search for Healing

The deeply hurting person tends to search for healing in a desperate fashion. The quest can become an all-consuming passion. Many people find themselves in a situation much like that of an Old Testament character named Naaman. Naaman was a highly respected leader, valued greatly by his master. He had been used by God and was a mighty man of valor (see 2 Kings 5:1). At first glance his life seemed wonderful—until we read that Naaman had a dreaded disease called *leprosy.*

Although Naaman was a mighty man, lauded as a great warrior and leader, his worldly power could not change his leprosy. Naaman felt utterly hopeless and believed healing was impossible.

Like Naaman, have you ever felt utterly hopeless? Have you ever reached the point where no hope of change seemed possible in your future? If so, describe what lead you to that conclusion and how you felt.

_____

_____

Hope Enters Naaman's Life

Hope springs from the most unexpected places. Many times in our desperate search for help, we overlook God's direction because it's so unusual, unexpected, or even because it appears so insignificant. Naaman encountered just such a time: "Now bands from Aram had gone out and had taken captive a young girl from Israel, and she served Naaman's wife. She said to her mistress, 'If only my master would see the prophet who is in Samaria! He would cure him of his leprosy' " (2 Kings 5:2, NIV).

Many times we overlook God's direction because it's unusual, unexpected, or even appears to be insignificant.

Never believing that hope could come from such an unimportant source, Naaman no doubt felt tempted to ignore the advice. This brave young girl pointed her master to the only solution available. Fortunately, it often takes only a little encouragement to someone desperate for healing! A few simple words from a slave girl and Naaman hurried to the land of Israel.

Like the servant girl, you can offer hope to those experiencing discouragement or depression. A few simple words of encouragement, a listening ear, or a hug can encourage one in deep pain to persevere a little longer. Our words, even without our knowledge, can motivate someone to a more sustained healing. This week, can you commit to encourage someone?

From the list below choose at least one action you will perform this week for a discouraged person. Place a check mark beside the action to mark your commitment.

❑ a phone call   ❑ a written note

❑ a simple act of service   ❑ a token gift of care

❑ an embrace or pat on the back

Healing Comes in an Unusual Way

Naaman apparently headed directly to the servant girl's homeland. After some interaction with the king of Israel, Naaman was directed to Elisha the prophet (see vv. 8-9). When he arrived at Elisha's home, Naaman received unexpected directions for his healing. Naaman was angry at the instructions (see vv. 10-11). Anger is a curious response from one so desperate to be healed. Just what made Naaman so furious? Read verses 11-13 to identify the sources of his anger.

1. He expected a particular person to be the instrument of healing. Verse 10 states that Elisha sent a messenger to Naaman rather than going himself. Perhaps Naaman believed that as a powerful warrior and leader, he deserved a personal visit. If so, we might interpret his response as pride.

2. He expected a specific method to be used to heal the leprosy. Naaman thought Elisha would call on the Lord, wave his hand over the leprous spot, and heal him.

3. He disagreed with the way the healing should occur. He argued that the Syrian rivers were better than any of the rivers in Israel. He wanted Elisha to change the prescription for healing. As a result, he left in a rage.

4. Clearly, Naaman was willing to do "something great" to receive healing, but he was unwilling to do something simple or even humiliating.

Do you find yourself desiring or demanding that God heal according to your expectations? Expectations are hard to release. List some expectations you have about healing for the discouragement or depression that you are experiencing.

_____

_____

_____

_____

Healing Experienced

With the encouragement of his entourage, Naaman entered the Jordan River and dipped seven times as Elisha prescribed. After dipping the seventh time, his flesh was not merely restored but appeared as a young boy's skin (see v. 14). When God does a job—He does it well! Wouldn't you have loved to have seen the look on Naaman's face as he came up from the seventh dip and realized that his gnarled, destroyed flesh was perfectly restored? Undoubtedly he leapt and shouted for joy!

Naaman returned to Elisha (see v. 15) and voiced his belief in the Lord as the only true God. The healing was instantaneous and dramatic and indeed convinced Naaman of the identity of the true God of Israel.

The healing process was much slower for Matt, about whom you read in day 2. From the beginning of his depression, it took more than a year for him to recover. Whether instantaneous or prolonged, your healing will come as a result of God's grace. God has a perfect plan for you; not only will it be the very best for you, but your life will influence the lives of others. Truly there is hope for those who cling tightly to Jesus.

God has a perfect plan for you; not only will it be the very best for your life, but it will influence the lives of others.

Consider the following confession. If you can embrace it as your own, then pray it to God as a covenant with the Master.

Lord,

I, too, like Naaman have specific expectations about my healing. At times I have been frustrated if not angry at how You are choosing to use this discouragement and depression in my life. I have wanted to shout to heaven: "It is not fair!" "This should not be happening to me!"

Forgive me for trying to force You to heal or sustain me according to my ways. I submit to Your method and timing concerning healing. Thank You for forgiving me. Empower me to trust Your unseen hand. Amen.

If you have participated in this study in an effort to understand and minister to someone who suffers from depression, take time to pray for him or her. Ask God for healing, and ask Him to provide you wisdom to discern the needs of your friend(s).

DAY 4
Find an Encourager!

Purpose: To identify an encourager for support; to become an encourager to someone else

Passage: Read 1 Samuel 23:14-17 in preparation for today's study.

Everyone, at one time or another, needs encouragement from another human being. Yes, we said everyone! No one is so strong, so mature, or so spiritual as to be immune to periods of discouragement or depression. Today we want to look closely at a super saint who was in need of encouragement. Hold on to your seat—you won't believe who it was. Here are several hints.

1. He was a mighty leader of Israel.
2. He was a courageous warrior.
3. He defeated a giant that older men were afraid to confront.
4. He was described as "a man after God's own heart."

Have you guessed yet? Of course, you have—it was David! Who would have thought that a man such as David would have experienced discouragement? But that is exactly what happened to him. First Samuel 23:16 says, "Then Jonathan, Saul's son, arose and went to David in the woods and strengthened his hand in God" (NKJV).

God's protection did not prevent David from becoming discouraged. Verse 14 points out that Saul was in unrelenting pursuit of David and had no intention of ever giving up. Saul was like a lion who stalks his prey with an continual persistence and intensity. Saul was a discourager. Unlike an encourager who gives to you, a discourager takes from you.

Some people replenish us. Others drain us. During periods of discouragement and depression, we absolutely must learn to identify the "replenishers" and include them in our lives.

The following lists provide characteristics of both replenishers and drainers.

Who would have thought that a man such as David would have experienced discouragement?

Replenishers

You desire to be with them.
You feel better after spending time with them.
You are able to "be yourself" with them.
They offer you hope.

Drainers

You are sapped emotionally and spiritually when you are with them.
You feel weighted down or burdened after spending time with them.
You experience dread when you think of being with them.
You are not comfortable "being yourself" around them.

Do you have more "replenishers" than "drainers" in your life? We all have some of both. In the appropriate column below, list the names of those in your life who fall into each category.

Replenishers	Drainers
_____	_____
_____	_____
_____	_____
_____	_____
_____	_____
_____	_____

To experience more effective living, we must choose to spend as much time as possible with "replenishers" and as little time as possible with "drainers."

Characteristics of an Encourager

What does the Bible say about those who lift others out of their discouragement? Jonathan's life offers several key characteristics of an encourager. There are certainly additional passages in the Bible related to encouragers, but this story is a great starting place.

Encouragers love you!

Encouragers love you. David and Jonathan established a close relationship prior to David's bout with discouragement (see 1 Sam. 18:1-2). The first verse of chapter 18 provides a beautiful picture of the deep spiritual intimacy David and Jonathan shared. "After David had finished talking with Saul, Jonathan became one in spirit with David, and he loved him as himself" (NIV).

This type friendship is best developed with someone prior to becoming discouraged or depressed. Developing relationships in the midst of the crisis or problems is difficult.

Do you have any Jonathan's in your life right now? It is important to have at least one close friend (besides your spouse if you are married). If so, write his or her name in this space.

_____

If you do not have a "Jonathan" in your life, would you be willing to ask God for a close friend? Write out your prayer below.

_____

_____

_____

Encouragers discern those who are discouraged and go to them. Verse 16 says Jonathan "arose" and "went" to David in the woods. We do not know how Jonathan learned that his friend David was discouraged, but we do know what he did. He went to be with his friend.

Jonathan was proactive. He didn't send a messenger to David to say, "The next time you're in the neighborhood of the castle, drop in and I'll be happy to encourage you." Jonathan left the comfort and familiarity of his home and went to David. Meeting discouraged persons where they are is one key to effective encouraging. Although it requires time and energy from us, the reward is well worth the cost.

Meeting discouraged persons where they are is one key to effective encouraging.

**Do you know someone who needs a "Jonathan"? ❑ Yes ❑ No
If so, write below how you can take the initiative to encourage him or her.**

_____

_____

_____

Jesus, our Savior, exemplified the characteristic of an encourager when He "left" heaven and came to earth for us. It cost Him to come to us. The price was His life! When an encourager comes to us, in some ways they are reflecting the incarnation of our Master, Jesus.

DAY 5
Jesus Invites You to Come

Purpose: To determine to bring your problems to Jesus

Passage: Read Matthew 11:28-30 in preparation for today's study.

Invitations are routine in American culture and are issued for a variety of reasons such as birthday, anniversary, going-away, wedding, retirement, or graduation.

Today we will examine an invitation Jesus offers to everyone but that applies especially to those who are discouraged or depressed. Jesus' invitation has a specific audience. Only those who "labor and are heavy laden" are asked to come (Matt. 11:28, NKJV). At first glance, the invitation seems strange—certainly not the usual guest list for a dinner party. The invitees are the tired, exhausted, fatigued, weak, fragile, hopeless, and shamed.

Jesus wants us to come to Him regardless of our condition or state.

Jesus wants us to come regardless of our condition or state. Often we humans respond to one another in an opposite way. For the most part, our acceptance of one another is conditional. Yet in this passage, Jesus offers a personal invitation from the Creator of all to come to Him in all our exhaustion and weariness.

How will you respond to the personal invitation from our Savior? Before answering, think about what would prevent you from coming to Him. Check the reasons that apply to you.

❏ I don't want to admit weakness.

❏ Others may reject me.

❏ He doesn't know how I feel.

❏ I tend to believe if I'm not living right all of the time, something is wrong with me. I've got to straighten that out before I come to Him.

❏ I don't want to be considered "lazy."

❏ Other: _____

Consider this analogy: In your mailbox you find a bright, white envelope on which your name is painstakingly written. Eager to read the letter, you hurry into your house. While sitting in your favorite chair, you carefully open the letter. On the pearl-white stationery you read these words:

My Dear Child,
I so long to communicate my deep love for you. You are so important to me. I am aware that you are presently facing some very difficult situations that are draining you of all your energy. The problems of life are gnawing away at your hope like a jackhammer persistently hammering away at a broken sidewalk. Come to Me! Wait no longer! I offer you rest and replenishment. Please admit your exhaustion and come to Me. I look forward to our time together.

Lover of your soul,
Jesus

Decision Time

Do you accept Jesus' invitation to come to Him and rest? Circle your answer below.

Yes   No

If you are struggling with the choice, consider the following prayer.

God,
Admitting I'm tired and discouraged is so difficult. Help me to accept Your invitation to come to You and rest. There is no other answer to my situation but to accept Your invitation. Holy Spirit, empower me now to step out on faith and come to You to receive rest for my soul. Amen.

Learning from Jesus

Perhaps you are making this choice for the first time—to admit your weariness and hopelessness. Do you remember the first and second stages of the biblical change process? They are awareness and understanding. If you are in one of those two stages, don't concern yourself with what to do. Instead, simply tell Jesus that you want to learn from Him how to find rest for your soul. "Come to Me, all you who labor and are heavy laden, and I will give you rest. Take My yoke upon you, and learn from Me, for I am gentle and lowly in heart; and you will find rest for your souls. For My yoke is easy, and My burden is light" (Matt. 11:28-30).

Will you tell Him you want to learn from Him? ❑ Yes ❑ No

Ask Him to show you how to accept the easy yoke and the light burden.

Continuing the Journey

Well, you've reached the end—of the study—but only the beginning of your journey! Congratulations on your perseverance! If you've studied to understand and minister, we pray that your efforts have been worthwhile. If you've studied this resource in response to your own discouragement or depression, we have several expressions of our own hope for you.

First, we hope you have gained some insight into the attitude our loving Heavenly Father holds toward you. That insight includes the awareness that depression can be a physical ailment with medical causes and does not signal a lack of faith.

We hope you have broken through some of the isolating effects of depression and observed how many of God's finest servants have struggled with this foe. We encourage you to keep reaching out. The Holy Spirit will supply the courage and strength to find the support you need. If you have not participated in a group processing of this study, you've missed a significant benefit. Pray about participating in a study and support group where you can share your struggles and progress.

Next, we hope you have gained some knowledge about the five causes of depression: loss, anger, stress, medical problems, and poor personal choices. If you are like most of us, the reason for your situation is not grounded in any one particular cause. More likely each contributes in a major or minor way.

We hope this process has helped you to begin some steps of growth and life change. How wonderful it would be if we could complete a study and be well, but we know God did not make us that way. He created us to learn and grow. We hope this study is a part of your growth process.

Finally, we pray that you have discovered one of God's greatest gifts—*hope*. If you had a "hopestat," similar to a thermostat but measuring hope instead of temperature, our fondest wish for you would be that your mercury is rising. Life becomes more and more worthwhile as we discover hope.

As you discover that hope, you will realize this is the beginning rather than the end. A friend likes to describe life using a football analogy. He says, "Wherever you are in your life, it's halftime. You have the second half to look forward to. The score at halftime doesn't matter. Play the second half. Your hope makes the difference." Jesus is our hope. We'll look forward to seeing you at the victory celebration. It's called the marriage supper of the Lamb (see Rev. 19:9).

As you discover hope, you will realize this is the beginning rather than the end.

Where Do You Go from Here?

We all need to grow. None of us has "arrived." As you have worked through *Strength for the Journey*, we hope that you have come to understand yourself better. We hope that you have come to understand and love God more. We hope that you also have discovered areas in which you need to grow.

You may feel that you have done enough work in your recovery from discouragement or depression, or that you need to leave this subject for a while and return at a later time. We have provided the following exercise and the information that accompanies it to help you plan for the next stage of your growth.

> **Think about areas in your life in which you need to grow. On the following list number your top three priorities.**

___ Understanding the Bible
___ Memorizing Scripture
___ Developing your prayer life
___ Overcoming either anorexia, bulimia, or compulsive overeating
___ Building witnessing skills
___ Changing unhealthy relationships
___ Beginning the road to recovery from an addiction to alcohol or other drugs
___ Knowing God's will
___ Becoming a disciple maker
___ Caring for your physical needs
___ Other _____

Remember that character development and spiritual growth are not instantaneous. Worthwhile goals take time.

Additional Resources

The following resources are written in the interactive format you have used as you studied *Strength for the Journey*. All of these books are intended for group study along with daily, individual work. Determine a particular area in which you need to grow. Then use one or more of these resources to help you continue your spiritual growth.

To develop your skills as a lay counselor:
• *WiseCounsel: Skills for Lay Counseling* by John W. Drakeford and Claude V. King. This study teaches a basic 10-step counseling model. Participants learn to listen, guide behavior change, and interact appropriately in relationships. Member Book: 0767326156; Leader Guide 0767326768.

To build your self-worth on the forgiveness and love of Jesus Christ:
• *Search for Significance* LIFE®Support Group Series Edition by Robert S. McGee, Johnny Jones, and Sallie Jones (Houston: Rapha Publishing). This study continues your work of replacing the four false beliefs with principles of truth from God's Word. Member Book: 0805499903; Leader Guide: 080549989X.

To deal with the grief and changes following a divorce:
- *A Time for Healing: Coming to Terms with Your Divorce* by Harold Ivan Smith. This course helps minister to the crucial needs of adults experiencing divorce. Member Book: 0805498753; Leader Guide: 0805498761.

To apply a Christ-centered 12-Step Process to codependent patterns:
- *Conquering Eating Disorders: A Christ-Centered 12-Step Process* by Robert S. McGee, Wm. Drew Mountcastle and Jim Florence. (Houston: Rapha Publishing). Applies the proved Christ-centered 12-Step discipleship process to help you overcome either anorexia, bulimia, or compulsive overeating. Member Book: 0805499776; Leader Guide: 0805499784.

To help you grow in developing a healthy lifestyle:
Fit 4 (Nashville: LifeWay Press®). This program applies biblical insights and relevant nutritional information in a support-group process. **Fit 4** groups learn and practice healthful eating, exercise, and spiritual-growth habits.
- **Fit 4** *Plan Kit* Includes two copies of the *Facilitator Guide,* four group session videotapes, promotional/facilitator training video, *Nutrition Starter Kit,* and *Fitness Starter Kit.* 0-6330-0580-0
- **Fit 4** *Nutrition Starter Kit* This 12-week course includes a *Nutrition Member Workbook, Accountability Journal Refill Pack* and three-ring binder, *Wise Choices* **Fit 4** *Cookbook,* and lunch bag imprinted with **Fit 4** logo. 0-6330-0581-9
- **Fit 4** *Nutrition Member Workbook* 0-6330-2883-5
- **Fit 4** *Fitness Starter Kit* A 12-week course that includes a *Fitness Member Workbook, Accountability Journal Refill Pack* and three-ring binder, the **Fit 4** Workout video, and exercise bag imprinted with **Fit 4** logo. 0-6330-0582-7
- **Fit 4** *Fitness Member Workbook* 0-6330-2010-9
- **Fit 4** *Facilitator Guide* Contains group session plans for facilitating both basic courses. Two copies included in Plan Kit. 0-6330-0588-6
- **Fit 4** *Accountability Journal Refill Pack* Space to record meals and exercise activities for 13 weeks. Includes helpful nutritional and fitness information. 0-6330-0589-4
- *Wise Choices* **Fit 4** *Cookbook* Contains easy-to-prepare recipes, menu planning suggestions, a grocery shopping list, food terms, label-reading instructions, and snack suggestions. 0-6330-0587-8

Fit 4 Continuing Studies
- *With All My Heart: God's Design for Emotional Wellness* 0-6330-0583-5
- *With All My Soul: God's Design for Spiritual Wellness* 0-6330-0585-1
- *With All My Mind: God's Design for Mental Wellness* 0-6330-0584-3
- *With All My Strength: God's Design for Physical Wellness* 0-6330-0586-X

Fit4.com Web Site
Up-to-date nutritional and fitness information, calculators for health assessments, fun quizzes, recipes, and more. Features on all four areas of wellness.

To explore more of what the Bible says about our hope for the future:
- *Our Christian Hope: Bible Answers to Questions About the Future,* by David Dockery. This study shows what the Bible says about the judgment, resurrection of the body, and heaven and hell. Member Book: 0767334779; Leader Guide: 0767334787 Leader Kit 0767334833.

To understand God's will for your life:

• *Experiencing God: Knowing and Doing the Will of God* by Henry Blackaby and Claude V. King (Nashville: LifeWay Press). Find answers to the often-asked question, "How can I know and do God's will?" This study helps Christians discover God's will and obediently follow it. Member Book: 0805499547; Leader Guide: 0805499512.

To learn more about the Bible:

• *Step by Step Through the Old Testament* by Waylon Bailey and Tom Hudson (Nashville: LifeWay Press). This self-instructional workbook surveys the Old Testament, provides a framework for understanding and interpreting it, and teaches Bible background. Member Book: 0767326199; Leader Guide: 0767326202.

• *Step by Step Through the New Testament* by Thomas D. Lea and Tom Hudson (Nashville: LifeWay Press). This 13-unit self-instructional workbook surveys the New Testament, provides a framework for understanding and interpreting the New Testament, and teaches Bible background. Member Book: 0805499466; Leader Guide: 0767326210.

To help you learn to think the thoughts of Christ:

• *The Mind of Christ* by T.W. Hunt and Claude V. King (Nashville: LifeWay Press). This course is a serious study of what it means to have the thoughts of Christ and to renew the mind, as Scripture commands. Member Book: 0805498702; Leader Guide: 0805498699.

Group Facilitator Guide
For Small-Group Sessions

Scheduling the Course

Strength for the Journey includes nine weekly studies. Encourage members to participate in all nine weeks, plus the introductory group session. We strongly suggest you make this a closed group after the first or second session. Trust will not develop in the group if new members continue to join. You will find a group covenant on page 158 and instructions for the covenant process in the introductory session.

Reconsider if you are tempted to disregard the requirement for members to sign the group covenant. Experienced facilitators will tell you this is a critical part of the group process. Ultimately you cannot change, heal, or fix group members. You do them a great service as you encourage them to complete the work they need to bring growth in their lives. Making a commitment to the group often makes an enormous difference in a member's experience.

Because the group sharing is so vital, keep the size of the group small. We recommend no more than eight persons, especially for your first group. If you have multiple facilitators, organize more groups as needed. If not, begin a waiting list. A group will not be effective if it is too large.

Preparing to Lead

Preparation to facilitate a *Strength for the Journey* group entails two phases: developing skill as a facilitator and familiarity with this particular group/study. You do not have to be an expert to facilitate this group. Becoming a truly effective facilitator takes much time and experience, but with the Holy Spirit's guidance, you can do a good job and make a major difference in people's lives.

Developing the Skills of a Facilitator

We want to describe something of the ideal to which we aspire as facilitators. Do not become discouraged if you do not fully meet all of these qualifications, but do not take them too lightly either. Consider the art of becoming a facilitator like you would learning any other skill from painting portraits to playing golf. Everybody starts out as a novice. Every facilitator needs to grow and develop better skills.

First, recognize that the purpose of a facilitator is not to teach the content of the book. Group members must do their own homework for the process to be effective. A good facilitator helps group members to share what God is doing in their lives through the study and through the group process. The facilitator seeks to help people to feel safe and to share both their thoughts and feelings.

A facilitator serves as something of a referee. He or she protects members from one another and sees to it that each member is drawn into the group sharing. If one member of the group begins to dominate discussion, a good facilitator skillfully moves the sharing to other group members. If group members get off track and begin talking about other issues, the facilitator leads the discussion back on track. If members begin to give advice, the facilitator redirects the group. As a growing facilitator, you will need to concentrate on the following areas:

1. *Move the sharing to the feeling level.* Group members will often intellectualize the study. Instead of talking about their own depression or anger, they will seek to talk about others or ideas. Ask members to share what they are feeling. Help them learn to share "I" messages instead of "you" messages. As you facilitate groups, you will recognize the enormous difference between a group that shares from their heads and a group that shares from their hearts.

2. *Be prepared for people with needs greater than the group can handle.* Maintain a referral list of counselors to whom you can refer members. We strongly recommend that you read *WiseCounsel*, a study for lay counselors. You will find *WiseCounsel* and other supplementary resources listed on pages 150-152. *WiseCounsel* will provide guidance in four areas. It will help you to develop better listening skills. It will help you to identify the person who needs additional help beyond what the group can give. It will help you to develop a referral list, and it will help you develop the skills to make such a referral. If you make a referral, for both legal and spiritual reasons, always refer the person to at least two counselors and allow the person to make the decision. If you recommend a specific counselor, you make yourself liable in the event that the person should sue over any actions of the counselor.

3. *Avoid advice giving.* Giving advice is destructive both to the group and to members. No one in the group will ever have all the facts, so they do not have a basis to give advice. If you or group members give advice, the person may come back later and blame you. You make yourself legally liable if you give advice, and you teach the person to rely on you instead of relying on the Lord. Rather than giving advice, experienced facilitators learn to say: "John, we are not here to give advice, but to support you. We believe that if you keep studying and working, the Holy Spirit can lead you to the right choices."

4. *Encourage people to be accountable.* Emphasize the group covenant, not as a legalistic requirement but as a means to show group members how they need one another. If one group member does not come or does not do the work, the entire group suffers. Some experienced facilitators say, "We're glad you're here and we want you to come to group even if you have not completed the work in your workbook. However, if you have not done the work, we ask you not to share in the group." No one answer fits every group or group member, but make it your goal to encourage members to complete their daily work.

5. *Seek to build a spirit of love and spiritual commitment in the group.* Express concern for one another. Demonstrate active listening. Train members to listen and respect one another.

6. *Involve every member of the group.* If one member dominates the group, enlist his or her help. After a group meeting, ask him or her: "Have you noticed that

some members of the group are not participating? Would you help me to get them involved? Let's give them lots of time to talk." If a member dominates the group by telling excessive details of a story, you may need to ask: "John, you are telling what was happening, but what were you feeling at the time?"

You will find facilitating a *Strength for the Journey* group is one of life's great challenges as well as one of life's great joys. Your task will be to lead the group to function effectively. Make it your goal that by the end of the nine weeks the group will operate effectively with a minimum of interference from the facilitator. You may choose to present and discuss the previous six principles as part of the introductory session.

Preparing Yourself with the Contents

Familiarize yourself with the contents. Read the Introduction and the first week's lesson to prepare for the introductory session. The first page of each lesson summarizes the content for that week. Read as much as possible of the remainder of the book. The more familiar you are with the content, the more helpful you will be to group members as you overview the course and lead the group.

Each week this facilitator guide will give you suggestions for processing what you and your group members studied during the week. Adapt the suggested session plan to fit your situation. Be flexible. When discussion is flowing readily, stay with the topic, even if it means omitting the next activity from the lesson plan.

The suggested session guides are designed for a 60-minute meeting. If you have more than 60 minutes, spend more time on each activity. If you have less than 60 minutes, select those activities which best fit your group.

Look over the next week's lesson plan early in the week to formulate your thoughts for discussion times.

Facilitating the Session

Begin and end each session on time. Groups benefit from structure and predictability. During the session, seek to maintain an atmosphere of safety and caring for group members. Monitor the discussion and move to the next topic when you feel the group is ready.

Encourage group members to talk to one another rather than focusing on you. Share the leadership by redirecting a question to the group: "That's a good question, Susan. What ideas would you be willing to share with Susan?"

Give permission for group members to disagree. Our purpose is not to promote uniformity. Each person will have a unique personality and style. We are in the group to support one another, not to become carbon copies of one another. Allow differences to emerge without feeling you must resolve them.

Our purpose is not to solve group members' problems. Often the group is most helpful by offering care and concern rather than advice. Some issues are resolved only through time and effort. Sharing someone's pain may be more healing than offering a "quick fix."

Since this study is based on biblical principles, encourage members to use and read the Bible. Use biblical examples where appropriate and focus on attitudes and behaviors that are pleasing to God. Make prayer a significant part of each group session. At the same time, don't allow religious words, the Bible, or prayer to become a club to batter struggling individuals. Encourage "grace space" where fears, doubts, and spiritual struggles are acknowledged without criticism or judgmental attitudes.

Model the behavior you desire for group members. Demonstrate encouragement through eye contact and body language. Be authentic. Share from your own personal journey. If you are open about your own struggles, chances are group members will open up as well.

Help group members to identify and express their feelings in a comfortable way. Your comfort level with emotions will model acceptance for other group members.

Plan ahead and follow your lesson plan. Spontaneous changes may prove unwise. Remember that no perfect group facilitator exists and be patient with yourself. Communicating positive regard for others is more important than a well-executed lesson plan.

Evaluating the Session

After each session, spend a few minutes evaluating the session. Here are some suggested questions you might ask yourself:
1. Was anyone absent this week? Do I need to make a follow-up call or send a note of encouragement?
2. Did I create a feeling of safety for sharing?
3. Did I communicate acceptance and concern?
4. Did I manage the group time wisely?
5. Were group members encouraged to help and support one another?
6. Did I practice good listening skills?
7. Did one person dominate the discussion? If so, how did I respond? What can I do to encourage participation by additional group members?
8. Did anything totally unexpected occur? How did I handle it? What should I have done differently?
9. How did I point participants to God's Word?
10. Would I recommend someone from this group to lead another group through *Strength for the Journey?*

Introductory Session

Prior to the beginning of the nine-week study, offer an introductory session to accomplish these objectives:
- explain the purpose of the study;
- overview the content;
- introduce yourself as facilitator;

- distribute copies of *Strength for the Journey*;
- review the requirements for individual study and group sessions;
- secure a commitment to the group;
- assign the first week's lesson.

You may need to adapt the Introductory Session guide, which is designed for 60 minutes.

During the introductory session present the group covenant on page 158. Have participants read the covenant together and verbally agree to its provisions. Or, reproduce it and ask members to sign and return it to you.

Co-Facilitating

One of the best ways to train as a facilitator is by co-facilitating with an experienced leader. If you are facilitating the first *Strength for the Journey* group in your church, enlist a trainee as co-facilitator. You can divide the responsibilities according to your individual gifts and abilities. Some facilitators prefer both to give input throughout the session. Others divide the session plan and alternate leading activities. Still others have a primary facilitator and one who takes care of administrative issues, such as attendance, name tags and other printed material, weekday contacts and follow up.

Target Audience

Most churches have members who would benefit from studying *Strength for the Journey*. Check with your pastor, minister of education, singles minister, and adult department directors to identify potential group members. Publicize the study in your church bulletin and newsletter.

Consider the outreach potential of *Strength for the Journey*. Invite people from your community. This group could be an entry point for unchurched and unsaved adults. Place an advertisement in your local paper. Urge church members to distribute announcements to friends, relatives, and coworkers.

Ordering Materials

Order sufficient copies of *Strength for the Journey* in advance of your first meeting. Order your workbooks through the Customer Service Center at 1-800-458-2772; or you may purchase them at the LifeWay Christian Store serving you.

Group Covenant

To encourage a high level of trust, love, and openness in my *Strength for the Journey* group, I covenant with my group's other members to:

1. Make attendance at group sessions a priority.

2. Complete each week's assignments prior to the group session.

3. Treat information shared in the group as confidential.

4. Support other group members as they share. I will try not to give advice or pressure other persons to see things my way.

5. I will pray for myself, my group leader, and other group members.

Signed_____

Date_____

Introductory Group Session

Before the Session

1. Have available a copy of *Strength for the Journey* for each participant.
2. If members are paying for part or all of their workbooks, make arrangements for collecting the money.
3. Prepare a group roster or attendance sheet. Keeping attendance records allows you to follow up on absentees. Regular contact is essential to prevent dropouts. Often participants need encouragement to complete the course.
4. Prepare to overview the course and Week 1.
5. Duplicate copies of the Group Covenant found on page 158.
6. Arrange chairs in a semicircle. Arrange for a chalkboard or marker board, or attach tear sheets to the wall. Supply chalk and/or felt-tip markers. Place name tags and markers near the door.

During the Session (50 min.)

1. As participants enter the room, ask them to prepare their name tags and take a seat in the semicircle.
2. Begin the session promptly. Welcome everyone to the group. Open with prayer.
3. Ask each person to introduce him- or herself. Explain that there will be time for more sharing later in the session.
4. Invite participants to share why they chose to be a part of this study. Share your own reasons for participating in the group. Identify with group members' expectations. "I, too, am looking forward to. ..."
5. Clarify your role as facilitator. Point out that you are not the official answer-giver or fact-finder. Explain that you, too, are a group member, seeking support and encouragement in your own walk with God.
6. Distribute copies of *Strength for the Journey* and, if necessary, explain procedures for payment.
7. Ask participants to turn to the Contents page in their books. Give a brief overview of the study, using information you reviewed prior to the session.
8. Direct members to the Introduction on page 5. Ask one participant to read the Introduction aloud as members follow along, or you may read it aloud.
9. Ask members to locate week 1 in their books. Invite them to look over page 9 and read the objectives at the bottom of the page. Call attention to the weekly Scripture memory verse. Encourage the group to memorize each week's verse.
10. Lead members to look through the week 1 daily lessons. Explain that doing the lessons will help them feel more comfortable sharing with others.
11. Call for questions about the book or weekly assignments. Recap the importance of completing the reading and learning activities on a daily basis. Affirm the privacy of each member's book.
12. Instruct group members to complete Week 1 before the next group meeting. Announce meeting time and date if different from the introductory session.

Closing the Session (10 min.)

1. Distribute copies of the Group Covenant. Ask participants to read and sign the Covenant and to give it to you before leaving the room.
2. Ask for specific prayer requests and lead in a closing prayer.

Evaluating the Session

Spend a few minutes evaluating the session with your co-facilitator.

❑ Did I create a feeling of safety for sharing?
❑ Did I communicate acceptance and concern?
❑ Did I manage the group time wisely?
❑ Did I encourage group members to help and support one another?
❑ Did I practice good listening skills?
❑ Did one person dominate the discussion? If so, how did I respond? What can I do to encourage participation by additional group members?
❑ Did anything totally unexpected occur? How did I handle it? What should I have done differently?
❑ How did I point participants to God's Word?
❑ For what specific needs or concerns do I need to pray this week?

_____

_____

_____

_____

_____

Group Session 1

Who Gets Discouraged?

Before the Session

1. Arrange chairs in a semicircle. Continue to use name tags as you feel necessary.

2. Read and familiarize yourself with the "Symptoms of Depression" (pp. 23-24).

During the Session (50 min.)

1. (5 min.) Welcome participants. Check attendance. Open with prayer.

2. (10 min.) Ask one group member to read 2 Corinthians 1:3-7. Using the activity on pages 13-14, ask, How many times were *comfort* and some form of *suffering* used? Invite members to share how they have been comforted by God or used by Him to comfort others.

3. (10 min.) Ask a participant to read Psalm 42:3-4. Ask, How can the words of the ungodly and memories of past joys cause us to lose hope? (p. 18).

4. (10 min.) Refer group members to the week's summary on page 23 and ask them to identify one of the four Bible characters whose situation they most identify with: Elijah, Paul, the psalmist, or Hannah. Why?

5. (10 min.) Ask the group to turn to "Symptoms of Depression" (pp. 23-24). Direct group members to identify symptoms experienced by the four Bible characters that correspond to symptoms on the list.

6. (5 min.) Refer members to "A Self Test: Symptoms of Depression" (p. 24-25). Assure them you do not need to know their individual responses, but encourage them to share their reactions to the test. Use questions to motivate discussion such as, Were you surprised at your answers? Had your realized you were having trouble concentrating? Did you know you had lost weight?

Closing the Session (10 min.)

1. Allow time for individuals to ask questions, make comments, or share insights. Avoid being the "answer-giver." Model the role of a good group participant.

2. Ask members if they are working through the learning activities, keeping up with their reading. Encourage their participation in small-group discussions. Do not be critical. Simply evaluate participation and offer encouragement.

3. Call for prayer requests. Close with prayer.

Group Session 2
Hope: The Answer for Discouragement

Before the Session

1. Plan to omit some activities if you have less than 60 minutes.

2. Arrange chairs in a semicircle. Place name tags near the door. Check attendance as members arrive.

During the Session (50 min.)

1. (5 min.) Welcome everyone to the group. Open with prayer.

2. (15 min.) Say, At the beginning of Day 1 you considered how you may be limiting God. Ask: What makes your situation seem impossible? How did Abraham respond in his impossible situation?

3. (5 min.) Which of the emotions listed on page 31 do you find troublesome? Why?

4. (10 min.) Read 2 Kings 6:8-19. Invite group members to share times their "eyes" were opened to see God at work.

5. (15 min.) Point out that we can trust in God for strength when we are without hope. Read Isaiah 40:27-31. Affirm God's commitment to each person. Ask group members for testimonies of God's faithfulness when they were tempted to quit.

Closing the Session (10 min.)

1. Invite participants to share additional insights about hope they gained this week.

2. Answer any questions about the workbook or the group sessions.

3. Ask for prayer requests. Close with prayer.

Evaluating the Session

Spend a few minutes evaluating the session with your co-facilitator.

Group Session 3

Loss: Grieving Significant Losses

Before the Session

1. Contact your pastor to learn if he offers counseling and his procedure for scheduling appointments. Ask him to recommend Christian counselors in your area. Consider duplicating and distributing a referral list during the session. Always provide more than one referral source. If you recommend a specific counselor you make yourself liable in the event that the person should sue over any actions of the counselor.

2. Print the five stages of grief (pp. 45-46) on the chalkboard or poster board for display during step 2.

During the Session (50 min.)

1. (5 min.) Welcome everyone to the group. Open with prayer.

2. (10 min.) Display the five stages of grief adapted from those first identified by Dr. Elizabeth Kubler-Ross: 1) Shock: "This isn't happening"; 2) Anger: "I'm angry about…"; 3) What If? (bargaining): "What if I had done or not done this or that?"; 4) Depression: "I feel helpless/hopeless"; 5) Acceptance: "I have come to terms with my loss." Say, Think of a significant loss in your life. Ask, What stage of grief are you in at the present time regarding that grief?

3. (10 min.) Read 1 Thessalonians 4:13-18. Review the case study activity on page 47. Discuss how you would use the hope of the resurrection to encourage this friend.

4. (5 min.) Ask one or several group members to share a new goal they developed using the guidelines on pages 54-55.

5. (10 min.) Day 5 presented practical suggestions for helping others who are grieving. Ask individuals to share how they have helped others either immediately after a loss or after some time had passed. Are there any ideas presented in this lesson that they will incorporate when their next opportunity to help arises?

6. (10 min.) If you or someone else (whose permission has been given in advance) have personally benefited from individual, couple, or family counseling, tell about that experience. Do not ask members if they have visited a counselor. That information is private. Tell or distribute information about Christian counseling services and future marriage enrichment and support group opportunities in your church and area.

Closing the Session (10 min.)

1. Allow unstructured time for individuals to ask questions, make comments, or share insights.

2. Call for prayer requests. Close with prayer.

Evaluating the Session

Spend a few minutes evaluating the session with your co-facilitator.

❑ Did I create a feeling of safety for sharing?
❑ Did I communicate acceptance and concern?
❑ Did I manage the group time wisely?
❑ Did I encourage group members to help and support one another?
❑ Did I practice good listening skills?
❑ Did one person dominate the discussion? If so, how did I respond? What can I do to encourage participation by additional group members?
❑ Did anything totally unexpected occur? How did I handle it? What should I have done differently?
❑ How did I point participants to God's Word?
❑ For what specific needs or concerns do I need to pray this week?

_____

_____

_____

_____

_____

Group Session 4

Loss: The Place I Called Home

Before the Session

1. Write on the chalkboard the Six Characteristics of Healthy Families (pp. 60-62), or duplicate them for use.

   • *In a healthy family, parents have an intimate marriage.*
   • *A healthy family permits you to be yourself and accepts you as such.*
   • *Healthy families practice open communication.*
   • *Healthy families share encouragement and affirmation.*
   • *A healthy family makes home a safe place.*
   • *Healthy families view conflict as a part of normal family life.*

During the Session (50 min.)

1. (5 min.) Welcome everyone to the group. Open with prayer.

2. (10 min.) Read Deuteronomy 6:5-9. Using the activity on page 60, ask group members to share how many of the principles in Deuteronomy 6 were present in their families.

3. (10 min.) Point to the Characteristics of Healthy Families (pp. 60-62) which you prepared earlier. Invite group members to share the extent to which these characteristics were experienced in their homes as children.

4. (10 min.) Refer group members to the first exercise of Day 4 (pp. 68-69). Ask members to share how much the past has affected them either positively or negatively. Refer to the last exercise (p. 69) and poll members to see which Present Indicators of Past Family Pain were checked most frequently:

Place a check mark by those thoughts most common to you.
❑ Others' feelings are more important than my own.
❑ I am worthless and unlovable.
❑ Bad love is better than no love at all.
❑ If people I care about reject me, I must be unlovable.
❑ I must be dependent on others or I won't survive.
❑ If I am good I will be loved.
❑ I am responsible for the behavior and feelings of others.
❑ I am responsible for making others change.
❑ I cannot trust anyone but myself.
❑ I am bad if I feel angry.
❑ I must keep peace at all costs.
❑ I can never change.
❑ I can never make mistakes.

5. (10 min.) Read Hebrews 13:5 to the group. Emphasize that God promises He will never leave us alone. Ask for volunteers to share their findings in the first exercise of Day 5 (p. 72) concerning God's abiding presence.

6. (5 min.) Ask each group member to turn to the last exercise of Day 5 (p. 73). Instruct them to review the list of those who have hurt them. Pray personally or ask a volunteer to pray for the group as a whole concerning forgiveness.

Closing the Session (10 min.)

1. Allow time for members to share joys, crises, breakthroughs, or other events from the past week.

2. Call for prayer requests. Close with prayer.

Evaluating the Session

Spend a few minutes evaluating the session with your co-facilitator.

❑ Did I create a feeling of safety for sharing?
❑ Did I communicate acceptance and concern?
❑ Did I manage the group time wisely?
❑ Did I encourage group members to help and support one another?
❑ Did I practice good listening skills?
❑ Did one person dominate the discussion? If so, how did I respond? What can I do to encourage participation by additional group members?
❑ Did anything totally unexpected occur? How did I handle it? What should I have done differently?
❑ How did I point participants to God's Word?
❑ For what specific needs or concerns do I need to pray this week?

_____

_____

_____

_____

_____

Group Session 5

Anger: When Anger Leaves Me Depressed

Before the Session

1. Write the three biblical principles concerning anger (pp. 76-77) on the chalkboard or prepare handouts.

   Anger is a powerful emotion and we need to exercise self-control.
   Anger should not be our most prominent personality characteristic.
   We should be angry in some circumstances.
   • When God's righteousness is compromised
   • When innocent people suffer

2. Provide slips of paper and pencils for use during the closing prayer time.

During the Session (55 min.)

1. (15 min.) Ask the group to suggest other Scripture passages that support the three biblical principles for anger. Allow time for discussion.

2. (5 min.) Ask group members to read Ephesians 4:26-27 and discuss their reactions to the idea that anger can be a positive thing (p. 79).

3. (10 min.) Refer to the list of ways that "anger turned outward" can contribute to discouragement (pp. 81-82). Ask group members to share other ways they listed that "anger turned outward" contributes to discouragement and depression.

4. (20 min.) Read Romans 8:31-39. Discuss answers to questions in the learning activity concerning this passage (p. 84). Ask group members to give examples of how family, school, and even negative church experiences can result in "anger turned inward."

5. (5 min.) Read Romans 8:1. Ask group members to share how this passage affects their regard for both themselves and other Christians.

Closing the Session (5 min.)

1. Remind members to complete the Self-assessment of Anger (pp. 88-89) if they have not already done so.

2. Ask for prayer requests. Distribute slips of paper and ask members to record one prayer request to remember during the week. Close the session by praying for one another, or you may pray for each member by name.

Evaluating the Session

Spend a few minutes evaluating the session with your co-facilitator.

- ❏ Did I create a feeling of safety for sharing?
- ❏ Did I communicate acceptance and concern?
- ❏ Did I manage the group time wisely?
- ❏ Did I encourage group members to help and support one another?
- ❏ Did I practice good listening skills?
- ❏ Did one person dominate the discussion? If so, how did I respond? What can I do to encourage participation by additional group members?
- ❏ Did anything totally unexpected occur? How did I handle it? What should I have done differently?
- ❏ How did I point participants to God's Word?
- ❏ For what specific needs or concerns do I need to pray this week?

_____

_____

_____

_____

_____

Group Session 6

Controlling Your Anger

Before the Session

1. Make copies of the Action Plan (pp. 97-98).

   An action must be clear and focused. Use the following form to develop an action plan.

   I need to speak with _____ about the following problem.

   1. What did the person do or say that made you angry or hurt?

   _____

   _____

   2. What sort of changes are you hoping to see?

   _____

   _____

   3. What might be the result if the situation does not change?[1]

   _____

   _____

During the Session (50 min.)

1. (5 min.) Welcome everyone to the group. Begin with prayer, asking God to help each one in the group with the difficult task of learning to control anger.

2. (10 min.) Ask for someone to explain the difference between how the aggressive person and the passive person expresses anger as presented in Day 1 (pp. 91-92). Take time for discussion.

3. (10 min.) Ask for a volunteer to read 2 Timothy 2:22. Using the first exercise of Day 2, ask group members to share their ideas on limits that they will not cross, "When I start to get angry I will _____." (p. 94).

4. (15 min.) Ask a group member to read Proverbs 15:1. Distribute the action plans. Being careful not to use names, ask group members to identify situations and help one another with ideas for an action plan.

5. (10 min.) Read Leviticus 19:17-18. Encourage participants to consider any names they may have listed in the first exercise of Day 5 (p. 102). Read Romans 12:20-21. Ask members to determine if they might do anything good for one or more of these individuals. Consider the ideas suggested in the lesson.

Closing the Session (10 min.)

1. Call for prayer requests.

2. Direct members to pray silently about the action they most need to plan or take in their lives this week. Ask them to pray specifically for the member on their left or right during the week. Close with prayer.

Evaluating the Session

Spend a few minutes evaluating the session with your co-facilitator.

Group Session 7

Stress and the Role of Health

Before the Session

1. Print the five possible causes of depression on the chalkboard or poster board to use to introduce the group to the week's study. (If you prefer, prepare handouts for steps 1 and 2.)

• Loss	Weeks 3-4
• Anger	Weeks 5-6
• Stress	Week 7
• Medical Problems	Week 7
• Personal Sin	Week 8

2. Print the four keys to balanced living (p. 118) on the chalkboard or poster board.

   • Live by faith in Jesus Christ.
   • Live by the Word of God.
   • Live according to your priorities.
   • Live for your goals.

During the Session (55 min.)

1. (5 min.) Welcome everyone to the group. Open with prayer.

2. (5 min.) Point to the "The Causes of Depression" list (?). Remind members that loss and anger were covered in Weeks 3-6. Stress and medical problems are today's topics. Personal sin will be discussed next week.

3. (15 min.) Ask individuals in your group(s) to share their answers to the first exercise of Day 1 (p. 106). Turn to the last exercise of Day 1 (p. 107) and ask the group to pray for individuals facing ill health at this time. Ask, Are there any practical things you can do to share God's comfort?

4. (30 min.) Refer the group(s) to the chalk board or list from Day 5 and the section entitled "Consider the Four Keys to Balanced Living" (pp. 118-121).

   a. Ask different individuals to read each verse and share answers to the first exercise.

   b. Ask individuals to share what has helped them to regularly read their Bibles. Allow time for sharing suggestions.

c. Ask individuals to share how God has helped them identify priorities or to face difficulties.

d. Share goals and pray together for group members' accomplishments.

Closing the Session (5 min.)

1. Debrief other group issues or concerns.

2. Share prayer requests. Ask for volunteers to lead in sentence prayers for these expressed needs. Close with prayer.

Evaluating the Session

Spend a few minutes evaluating the session with your co-facilitator.

Group Session 8

Poor Personal Choices: When My Sin Leaves Me Discouraged

Before the Session

1. Prepare a handout listing the three points of Genesis 50:20 from day 4 (p. 130) or list on the chalkboard.

   - Their Plan: You meant evil against me,
   - God's Plan: but God meant it for good
   - God's Purpose: in order to bring about this present result.

2. Review the message of the gospel at the beginning of day 3 (pp. 128-129). Be prepared to share it with the group, or call a group member ahead of time so that he or she can be ready to share it.

During the Session (50 min.)

1. (5 min.) Welcome everyone to the group. Open with prayer.

2. (10 min.) Read Genesis 50:20. Refer members to the chalkboard or the prepared handout. Ask for volunteers to share an experience where someone may have purposely tried to hurt them but God worked it out for good in their lives.

3. (10 min.) Read 2 Corinthians 7:8-13. Ask members to share their answers to the last exercise on day 1 (p. 124). Ask, Have you have experienced a situation similar to the Corinthians? Allow a volunteer to describe his or her experience.

4. (15 min.) Ask the group turn to day 4 (p. 128). Either share or ask the preenlisted group member to share the simple message of the gospel. Discuss the first and second surprises of the story of the prodigal son. Direct group members to list the loving actions of the father and describe three ways their Heavenly Father has blessed them beyond their expectations.

5. (10 min.) Take time to consider the question, "What Does It Mean to Forgive?" Read the illustration, "Will I Ever Forget?" (pp. 132-133). Review the three key components to acceptance, and ask group members to consider an individual(s) whom they have not yet forgiven. Lead the group in a prayer.

Closing the Session (10 min.)

1. Provide unstructured time for individuals to discuss issues not mentioned in today's study. Encourage others to offer support. Close with prayer.

Group Session 9

Hope for Today!

Before the Session

1. Since this is the final week of this study, prepare to share information at the end of the session concerning additional study opportunities available through your church in the coming weeks. You may refer to the additional study resources on page 150-152.

2. Prepare to lead a brief review of weeks 1-8.

3. Note that the session plan calls for 15 minutes instead of the usual 5-10 to close the session.

During the Session (45 min.)

1. (15 min.) Open with prayer. Lead a review of weeks 1-8 by asking members to turn to the introductory page of each week and review the daily lesson titles and objectives. Lead the group to recall each week's highlights. Give a one-sentence review of each week.

2. (5 min.) Ask members to turn to the introduction of week 9. Say, Think back to your first day in this group. How have you changed or grown during these weeks?

3. (10 min.) Ask for volunteers to share where they are in the Biblical Change Process (p. 139). What will they need to do to continue the process?

4. (10 min.) Review day 5 (p. 147) by asking the group to reflect on how during this study they have seen Jesus inviting them to come to Him for rest. Encougrage them to share glimpses they have had into God's plan for their future.

5. (5 min.) Repeat this week's Scripture memory verse together. Emphasize that as we hope for what we can't see, God's Spirit will help us in our human weaknesses.

Closing the Session (15 min.)

1. Present information about additional studies that will be offered during the coming weeks.

2. Thank the group for their participation. Affirm their openness to God's leading on their journey with Him. Use encouraging words to inspire further growth.

3. Ask individuals to consider facilitating a *Strength for the Journey* group and to let you know of their availability.

4. Ask the group to stand in a circle and join hands. Invite members to share one-sentence testimonies affirming the group and individual members. Invite volunteers to pray sentence prayers, and then close with your own prayer. Leave with hugs, handshakes, or other appropriate expressions of affection.

Evaluate the Group Experience

Spend a few minutes evaluating the session and the entire group experience with your co-facilitator. What can you do to improve the group experience the next time you lead a group. Pray about leading another *Strength for the Journey* group. Record your thoughts below:

_____

_____

_____

_____

_____

_____

_____

_____

_____

_____

CHRISTIAN GROWTH STUDY PLAN

In the **Christian Growth Study Plan (formerly Church Study Course),** this book *Strength for the Journey: A Biblical Perspective on Discouragement and Depression* is a resource for course credit in the subject area Personal Life of the Christian Growth category of plans. To receive credit, read the book, complete the learning activities, show your work to your pastor, a staff member or church leader, then complete the following information. This page may be duplicated. Send the completed page to:

Christian Growth Study Plan
One LifeWay Plaza; Nashville, TN 37234-0117
FAX: (615)251-5067
Email: cgspnet@lifeway.com

For information about the Christian Growth Study Plan, refer to the Christian Growth Study Plan Catalog. It is located online at *www.lifeway.com/cgsp*. If you do not have access to the Internet, contact the Christian Growth Study Plan office (1.800.968.5519) for the specific plan you need for your ministry.

Strength for the Journey: A Biblical Perspective on Discouragement and Depression
COURSE NUMBER: CG-0478

PARTICIPANT INFORMATION

Social Security Number (USA ONLY-optional) Personal CGSP Number* Date of Birth (MONTH, DAY, YEAR)

Name (First, Middle, Last) Home Phone

Address (Street, Route, or P.O. Box) City, State, or Province Zip/Postal Code

Please check appropriate box: ❑ Resource purchased by self ❑ Resource purchased by church ❑ Other

CHURCH INFORMATION

Church Name

Address (Street, Route, or P.O. Box) City, State, or Province Zip/Postal Code

CHANGE REQUEST ONLY

☐ Former Name

☐ Former Address City, State, or Province Zip/Postal Code

☐ Former Church City, State, or Province Zip/Postal Code

Signature of Pastor, Conference Leader, or Other Church Leader Date

*New participants are requested but not required to give SS# and date of birth. Existing participants, please give CGSP# when using SS# for the first time. Thereafter, only one ID# is required. **Mail to:** Christian Growth Study Plan, One LifeWay Plaza, Nashville, TN 37234-0117. Fax: (615)251-5067.

Rev. 3-03